Occupy Everything
Reflections on Why It's Kicking Off Everywhere

**Edited by Alessio Lunghi
and Seth Wheeler**

<.:.MinOr.:.>
.cOmpOsitiOns.

ACKNOWLEDGEMENTS

We would like to thank Stevphen Shukaitis, Emma Dowling, David Harvie, Ben Lear, Alex Andrews, Alice Nutter, Fergus Jenkins, Brian Layng, Katy Smith and Paul Mason for their unending help and patience in achieving this project.

This book is dedicated to Luca, Poppy, Katy and Frances.

Occupy Everything: Reflections on Why It's Kicking Off Everywhere
Edited by Alessio Lunghi and Seth Wheeler

ISBN 978–1–57027–251–6

Cover design by Alessio Lunghi
Cover photo © Yiannis Biliris www.greekriots.com
Interior design by briandesign

Released by Minor Compositions, Wivenhoe / New York / Port Watson
Minor Compositions is a series of interventions & provocations drawing from autonomous politics, avant-garde aesthetics, and the revolutions of everyday life.

Minor Compositions is an imprint of Autonomedia
www.minorcompositions.info | minorcompositions@gmail.com

Distributed by Autonomedia
PO Box 568 Williamsburgh Station
Brooklyn, NY 11211

www.autonomedia.org
info@autonomedia.org

You may ask yourself, well, how did I get here?

– Talking Heads

All that is solid melts into air, all that is holy is profaned, and man is at last compelled to face with sober senses, his real conditions of life, and his relations with his kind.

– Karl Marx

Contents

Introduction

Seth Wheeler & Alessio Lunghi

Penned in February 2011, Paul Mason's blog post "20 Reasons Why It's Kicking Off Everywhere" responded to the recent wave of student unrest, the European anti-cuts struggles, and what was fast becoming known as the Arab Spring. In his short post Mason offered 20 tentative forays into these globally disparate yet somehow connected struggles.

"20 Reasons" was warmly received within the social movements it commented upon, albeit not without criticisms. What resonated for us, was its lack of certainty as to where these movements were headed, and a pronounced distance from either ideological interpretation or "off the shelf" solutions.

It seemed that many in the social movements were content to carry on with business as usual, attaching longheld ideological certainties onto these developments. However some in existing activist groups, networks and organisations, began to question whether ideas, assumptions and certainties held from previous cycles of struggle could stand up to present challenges.

We saw "20 Reasons" as a chance to start an enquiry, a framework around which to better discuss our understandings of the present and as a means to gauge the effectiveness of movement responses to the crisis's facing capitalism and the nation state.

"20 Reasons" itself highlighted a series of political, economic, social, communicative and technological developments and suggested how these were being appropriated in struggle. The emergence of new or often ignored social subjects were also central to the piece – be that the "graduate with no future" or the socially excluded.

Understanding the present became an issue of importance and urgency for those interested in radical social transformation. As such, we commissioned a series of essays, responding to Paul's "20 Reasons", as a means to do just that.

In their opening essay, Thomas Gillespie and Victoria Habermehl, active in the Leeds University Occupation and part of the Really Open University (an ongoing project concerned with the transformation of the University from a neo-liberal model to a space held in common), explore the motivations and revolutionary potential of "The Graduate with No Future".

In "The Revenge of the Remainder", Nic Beuret and Camille Barbagallo expand on this in their discussion of the precariousness of life in contemporary capitalism. Written before the riots in England in August 2011, the authors outline a shift in the role of the unemployed/underemployed in capitalist development. Reserved – historically – as an army of surplus labour, they suggest that the "remainder" are increasingly excluded from even this role, with little or no opportunity for work and relegated now to the role of consumer or as the mere object of state-initiated control methods.

In their contribution, "On Fairy Dust and Rupture", The Free Association, an ongoing anti-capitalist writing project, ask how an insurrection might resonate beyond its point of origin. They attempt to develop a materialist understanding of the role of chance in social movements, which might help us "to conjure up something beyond ourselves, something we can't wholly know, something beyond the existing 'natural' limits of society; something 'supernatural'."

Much has been made of the so called Twitter/Facebook revolution by the professional media, in their accounts of 2011's unfolding struggles. And it is certain that social media played an active role in the dissemination of dissent. The Deterritorial Support Group (who describe themselves as "ultra-leftist" and as a "think-tank") explore the revolutionary potential of those who have grown up immersed in online culture. Their essay "All the Memes of Production" considers the role of the meme and online cultures of solidarity and their real world applications.

In "If You Don't Let Us Dream, We Won't Let You Sleep?", Ben Lear and Raph Schlembach (editors of the journal *Shift*) explore the failure of capitalism to deliver upon its promises of unending growth. Critical of the defensive positions undertaken by many in the anti-austerity movements, they argue for a robust engagement within present struggles, informed by the demand for "luxury for all" and not for a return to the world as it was before the crisis.

David Robertshaw, Rohan Orton and Will Barker (from the writing collective 500 Hammers) consider the failure of ideologies to attach themselves to real world events. In "Ideology Fail", they argue that the digital age has heralded a significant change in how ideas are both disseminated and received.

In a second contribution entitled "Fear and Loathing", the same authors also consider whether young radicals really have lost their fear and really can pick and choose their battles as Paul Mason suggests.

Antonis Vradis (a contributor to the blog Occupied London) reports from Greece, suggesting that all facets of social resistance, from the mobilisations against police brutality to struggles in the workplace have merged into each other in "A Funny Thing Happened on the Way to the Square".

In "The Revolution is my Boyfriend", Tabitha Bast and Hannah Mcclure (Leeds Space project, New Weapons Reading Group) consider leadership in the new movements, paying particular attention to the role of gender.

Andre Pusey and Bertie Russell (Really Open University) reflect on contemporary conceptualisations of power in their analysis of present forms of class composition, management and capitalist accumulation in their essay, "Do the Entrepreneuriat Dream of Electric Sheep?"

Federico Campagna (a member of the journal *through europe*) considers what tactics and conceptual tools are open to popular movements in their attempts to avoid military/state repression in his essay "Radicalising the Armed Services".

The final contribution addresses the caveats Paul Mason makes to his "20 Reasons". In "Some Complications... and their Political Economy", Emma Dowling looks at the present crisis of social reproduction and assesses the ramifications of the state and capital's recuperation of movements for autonomy and self-organisation. In the context of the UK, she confronts the Big Society beyond its rhetoric and analyses the wider interplay between austerity and market expansion as a front-line for contemporary struggles and collective organisation.

Inevitably, this short collection of essays provokes more questions than it can possibly answer. But questions are often more desirable than firm solutions, especially in the realm of politics. History is littered with the tragedies of those who put blind faith and certainty ahead of challenging their own assumptions. Inquiry opens up alternative pathways, elicits tactics and provokes future strategies not previously considered: "asking questions as we walk", as the Zapatistas say.

If we are certain of anything, it is that the very history that was declared to have reached an end is alive again. Once many believed "it was more possible to imagine the end of the world than the end of capitalism" – we wish to report that the future now seems more uncertain. Again, the possibility to imagine and construct a life outside of capitalism seems both realistic and vital.

On the graduate with no future

Thomas Gillespie & Victoria Habermehl

On November 10th, 2010 approximately 50,000 students marched in London against the British government's plan to slash funding for education. The march took the authorities by surprise when it deviated from its planned route and led to an occupation of the ruling Conservative party's headquarters. This event was followed by months of sustained militant action throughout the UK, with marches, strikes, occupations and happenings breaking out across campuses and cities on an almost daily basis. Participants did not belong to a single party, organisation or campaign. Rather, they comprised a diverse field of actors, many of whom had no history of militancy, who all appeared to have reached some sort of psychological breaking point. In what follows, we seek to understand why years of generalised apathy in the face of the strategic commodification of higher education in the UK suddenly gave way to this wave of mass resistance at the end of last year. We believe that this rebellion is driven by the growing perception that where once the university graduate had a bright future, now they have none.

This crisis of confidence in the university has been a long time in the making, beginning with the bubble of optimism created by the restructuring of higher education at the end of the Second World War. In the 1940s, '50s and '60s, successive British governments pumped huge amounts of public money into the universities in order to drastically increase the number of student places and to remove the financial barriers to studying through the introduction of universal grants to cover tuition and living costs. As a result, working class youths growing up in the second half of the 20th century had the opportunity to become socially mobile and access the higher echelons of the job market through obtaining a degree. Ploughing public money into higher education was justified on the grounds that the nation as a whole (and not just the individual graduates themselves) would benefit from the training of university graduates. Clement Attlee, Britain's postwar Labour Prime Minister, captured the mood of the time when he announced that:

> we cannot hope to solve our post-war problems unless we can increase the supply of trained men and women in the various departments of our national life. [1]

Opening up the universities to a wider cross section of the population was justified on the grounds that it was in the public interest to train scientists, engineers, doctors, dentists and teachers, not to mention arts graduates for executive and management posts in the private sector.

Today, this understanding of higher education as a public good is being eroded by the neoliberal tendency to extend market principles to all spheres of social life. Increasingly, a degree is understood through the lens of consumerism as a commodity to be purchased by an individual. Since the 1990s the public has incrementally reduced the proportion of the cost of degrees that it funds collectively via the state and the student has had to fund more and more of this cost as an individual through the payment of fees. When fees were introduced in 1998, students were expected to pay £1,000 per year. This rose to £3,000 in 2004. If the current government is successful in implementing their proposed public spending cuts then students will be paying up to £9,000 a year. In addition, maintenance grants have been replaced with repayable student loans for all but the very poorest students. When they first introduced fees and loans, Tony Blair's Labour government was following the recommendations of the 1997 Dearing Report, which argued that:

> those with higher education qualifications are the main beneficiaries (of higher education), through improved employment prospects and pay. As a consequence, we suggest that graduates in work should make a greater contribution to the costs of higher education in future. [2]

This report, and the resulting policy, clearly represented a rejection of the underlying logic of the post-war public university and signaled the emergence of a market rationality as the dominant organising principle in higher education.

This shift from public to private finance has triggered a corresponding and significant shift in the subjectivity of the contemporary student, i.e. the way that they understand themselves, the world around them and their relationships in that world. Since higher education is increasingly something that the individual must purchase at considerable cost, probably saddling themselves with tens of thousands of pounds of debt in the process, the decision to undertake a degree inevitably comes to be understood through an economic lens of cost-benefit analysis. According to the neoliberal rationality of higher education, a degree is only worth having if it will enable you to earn significantly more in the future than you would without such a qualification. This difference in earning power is often referred to as the "graduate premium", but it might as well be called the "profit margin". The consequence of this change in subjectivity is, as Jason Read has argued, that when they take a degree, students are acting like entrepreneurs who are making a capital investment with a view to generating a healthy return in the future. The university is interpreted, especially by those who attend it, as an investment in their human capital. Every class, every extracurricular activity, every activity or club becomes a possible line on a resume, becomes an investment in human capital. The question asked by every student at practically every college or university is: "how will this help me get a job?"[3]

The political implication of this shift in subjectivity is that the field of higher education becomes characterised by isolated, competitive, self-interested individuals who think of themselves as mini-entrepreneurs competing in a marketplace. Whereas the public university was funded on the grounds that it was a collective investment that would benefit society as a whole, the neoliberal university attracts funds on an individual basis from students who want to invest in themselves and their own market potential.

One of the flaws in creating an education system that encourages students to think like mini-capitalists is that capital requires a profitable return on its investment or else people will lose confidence in the system and it will go into crisis. This is exactly what is happening in the current environment of recession and austerity, as a whole generation of young people who personally invested in their education on the assumption that they would be rewarded with added earning power are graduating only to be greeted with indifference from potential employers. In early 2011, the UK Office for National Statistics reported the highest unemployment rate for those aged between 16 and 24 since "comparable records began", at 20.6%. Of those young graduates who do have a job, many have to settle for poorly paid and precarious positions in call centres, shops and bars rather than the professional graduate opportunities that were so abundant for our parents' generation. In those sectors that hold greater attraction to graduates – such as the media, or the so-called "voluntary sector" – there simply aren't enough jobs to go around.

How does the contemporary British graduate respond when they find themselves in this unenviable situation, accumulating interest on their student debt whilst pulling pints in order to (only just) pay the rent? Until recently, there has been nothing in the way of a collective political response to this disappointment. Rather, and consistent with the neo-liberal subjectivity of the contemporary student, we have witnessed the emergence amongst graduates of individualistic self-help strategies to try and get ahead of the competition in the constricting jobs market.

One such strategy is the unpaid internship. From the perspective of an economic subject who understands education as a personal "investment" in one's human capital, selling one's labour for free for several months makes a certain kind of sense. While the worker receives nothing in the way of wages for their labour, they are encouraged to think that they are, once again, investing in their own human capital by accruing work experience, references and contacts. It is on the basis of this capital that they will hope to distinguish themselves from their peers and, at some point in the future, get a return on their investment – a paid job in their chosen field. This strategy has worked for some graduates, notably the privileged minority who can afford to live and work in London for months at a time without earning any money. For the vast majority of graduates and their families, however, participating in such a scheme is simply beyond their means. As such, the normalisation of the unpaid internship since the 1990s has functioned as an informal social mobility filter, preserving the most sought after jobs for the wealthiest graduates whilst certain sectors of the economy clean up on free labour.

In the latter half of 2010, however, something appeared to be stirring. Why was the student body politic finally awaking from decades of slumber?

It could be argued that the wave of protest described above was somehow contiguous with the neoliberal rationality of higher education. Rather than challenging the commodification of higher education per se, perhaps the young are people merely demanding better value degrees (lower fees) and a better return on their investment (growth, jobs). Undoubtedly this is probably the case for some of the protesters. However, and while we do not claim to speak for everyone, we argue that there is an emerging network of groups who are actively trying to create a "new"university that breaks with both the post-war-public and neoliberal-private paradigms of higher education. While these groups were involved in the protests that swept the UK over the last months of 2010 and into 2011, they are also looking to move beyond the logic of protest to an affirmative politics of transformation within and against the university. Paul Mason understands these waves of protests as being based on a new sociological type, "the graduate with no future". As part of the group Really Open University (ROU), formed in Leeds in early 2010, we aim to challenge the current university system which reproduces this dynamic.

We understand the ROU as an ongoing process of re-imagining and transformation driven by a desire to challenge the higher education system and its role in society. Those involved explicitly reject the neoliberal model of higher education, where universities are run as businesses with students as consumers and where knowledge is a commodity that can be bought and sold. However, we also reject the notion that the era of the public university was a golden age that we should strive to return to. As discussed above, the public university served the interests of capital, rather than the common good, by reproducing the middle class sector of the workforce. Rather than a return to this model of higher education, we wish to see the creation of a free and empowering education system where creative and critical thought is fostered and knowledge is held in common. The ROU's praxis is summed up in the slogan "strike-occupy-transform". We engage in creative-resistive tactics that rethink and reclaim space, from flashmobs to public assemblies to autonomous educational activities. Through this process the ROU hopes to engage in affirmative struggle and, crucially, transform subjectivities by changing people's expectations of what higher education could be and what a university can do.

Motivated by similar concerns, the Lincoln-based University of Utopia argue that "we must dissolve the contemporary entrepreneurial university and reconstitute the university in another more progressive form". A pillar of their critical project is the reconceptualisation of the student "as producer". The neoliberal student who "invests" thousands of pounds in a degree thinks of themself as a consumer. The University of Utopia, however, seek to "reconstitute the relationship between student and academics – not as student as consumer, but as student as producer: students working in collaboration with academics as part of the academic project of the university". This understanding of student as producer informs the Social Science Centre, an independent, self-funded space in Lincoln where higher education courses are run on a cooperative basis, with students collaborating with teachers on course design, teaching and research. In the same spirit, the University of Utopia has also been successful in pushing for the introduction of more research-related activities to the undergraduate curriculum at the University of Lincoln, where its members are based. Student as producer signifies a break with neoliberal subjectivity through a shift in emphasis away from exchange to production – participating in education is about producing the common, not about purchasing a commodity.[4]

Members of both the University of Utopia and the Really Open University attended a gathering organised by the international Edu-factory network in Paris in February 2011. Groups and individuals from Europe, Tunisia, Japan, the US, Canada, Mexico, Chile, Peru and Argentina met to discuss and organise a network based on our common struggles around education. One of the key themes of discussion was the prevalence of precariousness, and the common statement issued at the end of the gathering called for the establishment of "a free university, run by students, precarious workers and migrants, a university without borders". This demonstrates that we are entering a new phase of struggle. Precarity is no longer something which workers must deal with on an individual level, as competitive elements in a job market. Rather, it is emerging as a basis for political organisation and class struggle on a global scale.

The emergence of this imperative to reject the old forms and rethink the university anew, taken together with the generalised militancy of the recent education protests, suggests that if the university graduate is beginning to reclaim their own future. This future does not lie in the intensification of competition, but in a collective rejection of debt and precarity, and in discovering new reasons to learn that cannot be subjected to an economic calculus of cost versus benefit.

NOTES

1   Quoted in Benn, R. and Fieldhouse R., "Government policies on university expansion and wider access, 1945–51 and 1985–91 compared", *Studies in Higher Education* 18, no. 3 (2003): 299–313.

2   NCIHE, *Higher Education in the Learning Society (The Dearing Report), Summary Report* (London: NCIHE, 1997).

3   Read, J., "University Experience: Neoliberalism Against the Commons" in *Towards a Global Autonomous University: Cognitive Labor, The Production of Knowledge and Exodus from the Education Factory.* (New York: Autonomedia, 2005).

4   http://www.universityofutopia.org/

Ideology fail

500 Hammers

"This is the language that has been wholly rejected across the world in every advanced society. This is yesterday's claptrap."[1]

When debating with Ken Loach over the Con-Dem governments proposed cuts to welfare and public sector services, Michael Heseltine made reference to the crowning achievement of neoliberalism. Not mass-privatisation of the few assets that the state had managed to seize before the 1980s but the successful sale of the idea that there was no more grand debate to be had, that, in the words of Peter Mandelson, "We are all Thatcherites now".[2] Anything less than supportive of the capitalist consensus shared by the political classes no longer needs to be attacked – it is simply ignored. If they condescend to engage with it then it is dismissed as fuzzy thinking, the folly of youth. The stereotypes of students, ivory tower academics and old left dinosaurs are unflatteringly contrasted with the business minded political pragmatists of the "real" world.

A steady decline in electoral participation could be regarded as one of the symptoms of this victory. The last general election saw a turnout of 65.1% among registered voters – less than half of the UK's total population.[3] If you're a true believer in the value of parliamentary democracy then that level of disengagement ought to be seriously worrying. Amongst non-voters there are those that regard the ballot box as a hollow gesture and the electoral system as a sham of democracy; whereas others would say that they believe in it as a system but that they are dispassionate about the outcome, trusting any of the candidates to suit their interests. Regardless of the underlying motivations of individual non-voters, electoral abstention echoes the widely perceived inadequacies of this way of collective decision-making. An alarming number of people are either unsupportive of the neoliberal consensus or sufficiently content with it that they don't feel the need to participate by deliberating over its managerial style.

We now have generations of people who find it hard to take elections seriously. Distrust and suspicion of politicians is the norm, and finding someone who unequivocally supports a particular political party is akin to encountering an evangelical Christian; both are strange and discomforting in their blind faith. Voting is no longer done to support something you believe in, it's a preventative measure that guards against the worst excesses of parties and policies that you oppose. That classic criticism of the disparate strands of anticapitalist politics, "you're only against something, you don't know what you're for", now makes for a fairly accurate portrayal of voting in parliamentary elections.

People interested in radically changing society could be forgiven for feeling despair in this situation but there are also reasonable grounds for optimism. Whilst the cheerleaders of neoliberalism refuse to admit that theirs is just another ideological position that could be superseded they also make it difficult for themselves to argue against their critics. It's something of a challenge to be a successful advocate for an ideology if you refuse to admit that it *is* an ideology in the first place. This means that anticapitalist positions can be reframed as reasoned and pragmatic responses to a problem. The terminology of left wing opposition groups – anarchists, socialists, Marxists etc – may well have been tainted with the insinuation that they are regressive or anachronistic but the ideas behind them are as strong as ever. As these ideas shed their baggage they sneak into the mainstream, occupying the gaps left by the crumbling mandate of the major parties. Full-throated support for Labour died after Iraq and the Liberal Democrats were wiped out in the local elections only a year into coalition. There is no party that can successfully muster any eagerness for themselves even as an alternative to the others. This means that any dissatisfaction with the status quo is inevitably pushed towards a politics that occupies a space far distant from the centre.

Despite lessons from history that warn of extreme nationalists' ability to capitalise on times of economic hardship it still feels rather difficult to take them seriously as a threat. They have made numerous attempts to realign their politics in recent years yet their focus is hopelessly out of step with the concerns people are expressing. Try as they might to make dubious connections, Islamic fundamentalism cannot be blamed for the banking crisis any more than eastern European immigration can be held responsible for public sector cuts. So the far right are now stuck in a tabloid-esque rut of making tenuous links between immigration, housing shortages, job opportunities and pedophilia.

> I'll tell you what right, we have no problem with mosques being built over here so long as we can build mosques in Mecca, I'd love to see that, I would love to see a mosque being built in Mecca.[4]

It is true that the English Defence League have got tens of thousands of followers on Facebook and that they have been capable of mobilizing a couple of thousand football casual/racist types for some of their events. But at their most worrying they are a minor threat to public order and their stance seems unlikely to evolve into anything remotely resembling policy. Their highly spun mission statement stands completely at odds with what the inarticulate punters that turn up to their events have to say about things, so they remain a highly confused angry mob. It seems at times that the counter demonstrations that are organised actually end up legitimising them beyond their real reach and provides the EDL with the conflict that they thrive upon. It would almost be more fitting to use interviews with EDL members to emphasise the importance of adequately funding public education than as a reason to worry about a rising nationalist tendency among the wider public.

Alongside the street presence of the EDL the more policy oriented BNP are running into trouble. The "debate" in the run up to the AV referendum saw both the "yes" and "no" camps making use of them as a bogeymen to scare people with and it would be foolish to ignore the fact that they have made some gains in the recent past. That said, these gains have failed to translate into seats other than at a European level and they have been offset by travesty after travesty. They've been publicly ridiculed on Question Time, uninvited to the Queen's garden party, had their members list leaked to the public and the courts have found their membership criteria to be incompatible with racial equality laws. In the aftermath of the 2010 election an ill-calculated leadership challenge saw expulsions and infighting that left a significant number of unfilled vacancies in their organisation. This was then topped off by an out of court settlement to Unilever that brought them to the verge of bankruptcy after their unauthorised use of the Marmite brand during a party political broadcast. Partly as a result of all this, the recent local elections saw them lose 11 of their 13 council seats.[5]

"I'M NOT YOUR COMRADE"[6]

At the same time on the left there is a sense of things changing. An increasing militant tendency is developing with widespread talk of strike action in various sectors, occupations from the Gaddafi mansion in Hampstead to over 20 university campuses, not to mention the largest Black Bloc in UK history. Younger people are coming to the fore, largely indifferent to the sectarian squabbles of previous generations. Although the infighting persists in some quarters, other groups have made moves that hint at the possibility of a sea change. Early in 2011 the Climate Camp network disbanded after 5 years of direct action against causes of man-made global warming with a recognition that as times have changed so too must they.[7] In doing so they also abandoned the somewhat restrictive nature of single-issue interventions. Equally promising was the refusal of the "good protester/bad protester" dichotomy by the UK Uncut spokesperson on BBC Newsnight in the aftermath of March 26th.[8] These may be small steps in the right direction but they are refreshingly so.

In the background to all of this it seems significant that our collective relationships with information and analysis are changing. In the past, when the large national news companies were the major outlets of information for what was going on in the world, it was difficult to find alternative commentaries on current events. The mainstream media has always implicitly supported the status quo: there may be scores of articles critical of a government or its policy, but the suggestion that representative democracy is a bad system is virtually non-existent. Specific companies can act in a corrupt or negligent manner, but capitalism itself is never put on trial. For a critical analysis of this kind it was necessary to go to the texts of fringe political parties and organisations.

Today the critical analysis often comes to you. The habit of linking articles on social media sites has created a situation where select pieces of information, from a wide range of sources are presented in a feed that is not only as wide-ranging as your own interests but as broad as those of your friends and contacts as well. Alongside a *Guardian* article or BBC page, there appears a link to an anarchist blogger, an article in the *Socialist Worker*, or maybe one from *Al Jazeera*. In addition to this, first hand accounts of the situation on the ground at major events are now routinely posted up on Youtube or Twitter and circulated within 24 hours. Amongst such a multitude of sources it seems to be difficult to commit to any one group or ideology. There are no longer any "classic texts", instead there is tendency of cherry picking ideas and information, of engaging critically with the material that is presented.

This barrage of information through an ever-changing series of connections stands at odds with outmoded ideas of a party line. The fluidity of the online world translates into impatience with the static nature of many groups in the physical world. As ideas flows more easily people learn to make connections and form and re-form groups almost seamlessly. The way information moves through the internet makes it difficult to hold on to a hermetic set of beliefs, it constructs people who would have difficulty even conceiving of such a thing. Of course there is the other face of that wealth of connectivity, the ability to surround oneself with those who strictly adhere to one's own ideology; yet this seems to be the exception rather than the norm.

This should not be taken as an argument that the internet will somehow solve all of our problems or that it is an inherently positive force. Whilst the reluctance to accept dogmatic ideology or tie oneself to a traditional party or group is refreshing, it sometimes comes at the expense of coherent group action. Knowledge may be power but power is useless unless it is exercised, and a struggle must move beyond information exchange and debate to activity in a physical realm. The collapse of rigid ideologies in the face of new forms of communication and thinking potentially presents us with new ways of forming mass organisations that that could retain a serious radical agenda among their members and take action in ways that previous broad church associations failed to do; Hopefully this can be achieved without them relegating themselves to the exclusive clubs of radicals, screaming from the sidelines.

NOTES

1   Newsnight: Michael Heseltine and Ken Loach, October 6th, 2010, available at http://www.youtube.com/watch?v=J6OLguh7_P8

2   Mathew Tempest, "Mandelson: We're all Thatcherites now", the *Guardian*, June 10th, 2002.

3   http://news.bbc.co.uk/1/shared/election2010/results/

4   "EDL Mastermind", http://www.youtube.com/watch?v=4v0GoMQvO0Q

5   "Vote 2011: BNP suffers council seat losses", http://www.bbc.co.uk/news/uk-politics-13313069

6   Heard at the Michael Sadler Lecture Theatre Occupation at Leeds University, http://leedsucu.wordpress.com/2010/11/28/leeds-occupiers-host-a-model-symposium/

7   "Metamorphosis: A statement from the Camp for Climate Action", http://www.climatecamp.org.uk/2011-statement.

8   Interview with UK Uncut, *Newsnight*, March 28th, 2011, http://www.youtube.com/watch?v=5IhS7yBcMnE

On fairy dust and rupture

The Free Association

It began with the suicide, a self–immolation by fire, of a man who has been downgraded to unemployment, and to whom was forbidden the miserable commerce that allowed him to survive; and because a female police officer slapped him in the face for not understanding what in this world is real. In a few days this gesture becomes wider and in a few weeks millions of people scream their joy on a distant square and this entails the beginning of the catastrophe for the powerful potentates.

– Alain Badiou, 2011[1]

Before, I watched television; now television is watching me.

– Egyptian rebel, 2011[2]

In the 1980s security experts in the West used the idea of the domino effect to talk about social movements in Central America. El Salvador, Nicaragua, Guatemala, Honduras: the US government feared that victory by "communist" (sic) forces would threaten its own strategic interests. If one government were allowed to fall to popular power, neighbouring regimes would topple, one after the other, until the spectre of revolution was at the gates of the US itself. Underlying the domino theory was the laughable notion that outside agitators (in this case, Moscow or Cuban trained revolutionaries) were somehow responsible for the rise of popular national liberation movements. But the domino theory was also part of a wider outlook that tries to squeeze social movements into a mechanistic

Despite the disappearance of the crisis behind the veil of necessity, we still feel something changed in 2008. It is hard to make out what that something consists of; it has, after all remained, largely mute. Opinion polls, however, continue to report sizeable proportions disagreeing that the free market economy is "the best system", even in countries such as the United States. With some analysis though we can begin to guess at its contours. The "natural" state of things once seemed to promise an improved life – if not for us then at least for our children. Now that promise appears empty and the "natural" state of things seems more like a trap. If the path to what we currently understand as "the good life" becomes blocked, then we can come to question whether it was such a "good life" after all. This is why it has been so hard to make out the something that has changed; it is a change in the underlying structure of contemporary desire. What we once desired, and the mechanisms that produced those desires, have lost their coherence.

This means that new desires are being produced and with them new political possibilities. We can be sure of this because of the change in recent struggles. We have seen the unexpected resonance of previously minority ideas. We have seen the emergence of the kind of movements not seen for a generation. We have seen cascades of events that have broken forty-year stalemates. Yet we still don't know how far the new possibilities go because they have not been given full expression. Only collective political action can do this and our task, if we have one, is to see if we can trigger it. The problem, of course, is that we are also caught, to a greater or lesser extent, within the current sense of things. As such we, as anticapitalist militants, are also sorcerers. We are trying to conjure up something beyond ourselves, something we can't wholly know, something beyond the existing "natural" limits of society; something "supernatural".

It is in conditions like these that concepts like fairy dust begin to make sense. Fairy dust invokes the need for a gamble, a roll of the dice, an experiment. For this we need to leave our safety zones. "'We don't know' thus makes us leave the safety of the regime of judgment for one of risk, the risk of failure that accompanies all creation."[8] But involving the element of chance doesn't mean just trusting to luck. We can think of the process of putting "a little bit of fucking fairy dust over the bastard" as a kind of incantation that draws on past experience in order to exceed it. Even the Troggs knew that the path to fairy dust lies between knowledge and cliché: "'I know that it needs strings, that I do know."

Given this, we can see the occupation of Millbank Towers during the demonstration against tuition fees as an invocation. That jubilant show of defiance as boots went through windows crystallised a new mood of militancy. By doing so it conjured up a movement no one was expecting. Yet that movement has stuttered as it has failed to generalise. Another example of actions sprinkled with fairy dust can be found with UK Uncut. Who could have predicted that occupations of Vodafone shops would resonate so widely and spread so virally? Was it the result of fortuitous circumstances? Or did the specifics of its incantations facilitate its spread?

UK Uncut certainly shows us some of the elements needed for a contemporary invocation of politics. Firstly it manages to capture a spreading desire to take part in direct action. There is a deeply felt need for a new collective, participatory politics to counter the parliamentary-democratic system's killing of politics. Yet UK Uncut's actions also spread because they are easily replicable. They have a low entry level. Taking part isn't too difficult. It doesn't require too much preparation or specialist knowledge. The risks involved are not too high. Secondly, although the actions contain a "supernatural" element, they also make immediate sense. The argument is instantly grasped: austerity is a political decision and not the result of a "law of nature". It is a political decision not to tax corporations and the rich as rigorously as the rest of us. It is a political decision to impose the costs of the crisis onto the poorest of society and those who did least to cause it. The UK Uncut actions, and the police response they provoke, reveal some of the dynamics of capital that neoliberalism seeks to deny. They reveal, for example, that capital contains different and antagonistic interests and that politicians, the police and contemporary structures of power align themselves with certain interests and against others. It is a political decision to do so.

Yet there is a danger here. Because actions must be instantly understandable, they can only push so far into the boundaries of what it is currently possible to say. They must by necessity still contain many of our society's hidden presuppositions to thought. If the actions don't contain a dynamic that pushes further and generalises wider, then the movement risks collapsing back into the sense of the old world. We are all too familiar with this. "Of course we'd love to tax the bankers", says the government, "but if we did they'd simply move to Geneva." The parliamentary-democratic system seeks to kill every revelation of a political decision with a new "naturalisation".

Now we can make out the third necessary element of our incantations. Our forms of action must include mechanisms or moments that set the conditions for collective analysis. Perhaps they must build in spaces, physical and temporal, which can maintain collectivity while slowing down the level of intensity. We need that familiar rhythm between the high intensity of action and the cooler pace of discussion and analysis. It's only by maintaining this rhythm that we can push further through the dynamics of capital that limit our lives. In such conditions movements can change and adapt in order to generalise. During the student movement the occupations played something of this role but on their own they weren't enough. For a movement to move, it must exceed the conditions of its own emergence. While a small group might stumble across a workable incantation, they must conjure up forces that make themselves redundant. The aim must be to make the mass its own analyst, to spread the potential for leadership across the whole of the collective body. After all if a genie gives you three wishes, then your last request should always be for another three wishes.

NOTES

The Free Association is an ongoing experiment loosely based in Leeds, in the north of the UK, although we find ourselves at home nowhere (and everywhere). www.freelyassociating.org.

1   "Tunisia, Eygpt: The Universal Reach of Popular Uprisings", at http://www.lacan.com/thesymptom/?page_id=1031.
2   Cited by Badiou, "Tunisia, Eygpt: The Universal Reach of Popular Uprisings".
3   http://bit.ly/wlmxrD.
4   The Invisible Committee, *The Coming Insurrection* (Los Angeles: Semiotext, 2009).
5   Two brilliant accounts of the 1981 riots are *Like a Summer with a Thousand Julys* (http://libcom.org/library/summer-thousand-julys-other-seasons) and *We Want to Riot, Not to Work*; Wu Ming 1, "We're all February of 1917", at http://www.wumingfoundation.com/english/wumingblog/?p=1810.
6   http://www.youtube.com/watch?v=En4ase-1-FA.
7   Phillipe Pignarre and Isabelle Stengers, *Capitalist Sorcery: Breaking the Spell* (Houndmills, Basingstoke, Hampshire: Palgrave Macmillan, 2011).
8   Pignarre and Stengers, *Capitalist Sorcery*, 44.

All the memes of production

Deterritorial Support Group

When Richard Dawkins coined the term "meme" in 1976 he drew upon his field of genetics and evolution to provide a rich metaphor for the way ideas, and systems of ideas, were transferred between populations. Rather than holding their form as they might originally be conceived by their author or originator, ideas changed according to their environments, developing to suit the needs of those using them, adapting to external conditions, much like a gene might. Based upon their suitability, universality or ability to shape-shift, ideas either took root and survived or died out. It remains a reasonably simple idea – for example, religions who held a degree of understandability, adaptability and universality spread quickly across the world, much as a virus might. Others, lacking relevance for those who came into contact with them, burdened by rituals which failed to touch their participants, died out, or existed only in small, homogenous populations.

Dawkins' lucid idea caught the eye of those with a particular interest in the field. Fittingly, however, it wasn't until we experienced a major change in the concrete conditions of the information environment that the idea of memetics really took hold. Prior to the invention and popularisation of the internet the meme was an interesting theory – today it's a conceptual tool without which our understanding of information transfer would be unable to function. More than this, the meme has become a self-conscious and self-reflexive idea; memes are called out at their birth, referred to as memes in their early life, become riffed upon until they reach a position of universality, or die, unsuitable for further use.

It is in the pervert's hothouse, online megafora 4chan.org, alternatively defined by FOX News as the "internet hate machine", that the most ubiqitous memes of internet history have emerged. 4chan.org, created by Chris Poole at age 15, functions principally as a imageboard[1] based on the Japanese model popularised by the Futaba Channel. 4Chan is home to 10 million regular users, with anonymity being the socially acceptable default. The most visited board on the site is the random – or /b/ board – the inhabitants of which are affectionately referred to as /b/tards.[2]

What sets 4chan apart from any other online community is not just its preference for anonymity or its anti-leader and anti-celebrity ethic but the sheer speed at which ideas, images and threads are generated, commonly referred to as the hivemind.[3]

A primary driver of memes within 4chan and within wider social networking is the concept of "lulz". A bastardisation of the plural of the popular acronym "lol"[4], lulz are essentially the *raison d'être* of the internet meme – an attempt to derive humour, usually through a joke of prank. But more than this – humour for its own sake, humour devoid of a moral framework. For the internet to crash into someone's lives, rip up their family photos and take a shit in their front room, and to find it funny. Lulz are more than a social glue for the fabric of internet society – they are an ideology, a be-all-and-end-all. For 4chan and the culture it has spurned, lulz are the embodiment of a certain corporate ethos – "EVERYTHING IN THE LULZ, NOTHING OUTSIDE THE LULZ, NOTHING AGAINST THE LULZ". To feel a twinge of sympathy for the victim of a raid[5] is not to engage in a moral discourse – it's to betray weakness, and unacceptable dissent against the ideology. It is to render oneself a "MoralFag".[6]

Joke memes (memetic lulz) operate by a continual development of the humorous content, adding more and more layers to the joke until sometimes the original source of humour has been totally removed. Instead, it's the referencing back to its own history that becomes the source of humour. However, with the need for the humour to actually *make sense* in relation to the content removed, the form itself becomes its own subject. Content unrelated can be added to this, picking up some of the cache of the original meme to ensure its reproduction.[7]

It is within this context of a completely amoral historical role that we must analyse the significant and under-critiqued change in internet culture in the past few years, then. From the "end-point" of total irony has developed a deviant culture – Anonymous, an online group engaging in online and IRL[8] political and social actions. Anonymous is a significant case study in internet memetics; and, importantly, in the move from a focus of lulz and life-ruination to an engaged and effective attempt at political organisation for the aim of radical social change.

The constituent parts of Anonymous are made up of a rapidly evolving framework of moralfaggotry, trolling[9], anonymously-authored action and lulz for lulz sake. Identifying the birth of Anonymous is in itself problematic due to the very nature of its name – existing as a vehicle by which any gathering of individuals can identify, whether for ethically motivated micro protest or raids for the sake of individual life-ruination. Perhaps this is best represented in the case of Jessi Slaughter, a Youtube tween, targeted for a raid in 2010, for her self-aggrandising yet naive videos in which she proclaimed to her haters "I'll pop a glock in your mouth and make a brain slushie". This quickly provoked rage in the 4chan community, resulting in a torrent of abuse, pizza orders and Jessi's home address being circulated online.

Attacks are typically carried out in the form of DDoS attacks[10], orchestrated with the tool Low Orbit Iron Cannon, coordinated through Internet Relay Chat[11]. LOIC allows a large group to collectively overload a site's server and bandwidth capacity, taking the site offline. Although most attacks are based in the virtual, typical tactics within raids attempt to make an individual or organisation's existence a misery through whatever means possible, be it unpaid take-away deliveries from every store in the city to their address or calling in bomb threats to a location where the individual organisation is known to be. Within the amoral frame of the rules of the internet everything is permissable, providing it results in lulz.

Prior to the poorly researched public outing of Anonymous as a known entity by the mass media (in an attempt to elucidate the cyber activities of the Wikileaks saga), the group has been responsible for countless hacktivist based political actions. Too numerous to detail in full, the most successful long term projects of the group are commonly recognised as Chanology (the ongoing cyberwar on Scientology) and Operation Titstorm: the attacks on the Australian government's websites and the targeting of individual politicians as a response to the government's attempt to censor the internet. Operation Payback targeted the MPAA (Motion Pictures Association of America) which was attempting the digital privatisation and enforced copyrighting of easily available online content, as well as repeated attempts to shut down the p2p torrent directory The Pirate Bay. It was Operation Payback that swiftly evolved to support Wikileaks during their disclosure of diplomatic cables, attacking Mastercard, Paypal and Amazon for their withdrawal of services from the organisation.

This marked the start of a difficult shift in motivational factors for Anonymous and the 4chan community. No longer were lulz the determining factor in actions– instead, in true meme-development fashion, another layer of meaning had entered the equation. As the populations of North African and Middle-Eastern countries rose up in (partly online organised) insurrection, Anonymous began to draw links between previous political actions, such as Operation Titstorm, which focused on the hacker-inspired defence of internet sovereignty and freedom of information, and its concrete relationship with IRL political change. The defence of Wikileaks, for example, could no longer be sustained as an autarchic, purely online action happening in a political vacuum. Wikileaks was having very real repercussions in Tunisia and Egypt, and it was at this point where Anonymous began a series of Operations, including providing advice for activists on avoiding state surveillance online, recipes for antidotes to tear gas, connecting video livestreams and info sheets lifted directly from the boards of 4chan. In the final instance, Anonymous worked to restore internet access via dialup connections and proxies to Egypt when the panicking regime "turned off the net".

The decision by Anonymous to undertake these actions was a result of its organisational processes. Due to its (nominally) non-hierarchical discussion process, combining polling and free conversation on IRC around the issues, and the consensus decision-making process, Anonymous could legitimately move as a group from taking action based on meme humour and start to take action as a response to human rights abuses and governmental repression, without cracking due to internal pressure, or under the weight of its own contradictions. Hackers could opt out, dissenting voices could be heard, but, ultimately, effective action could be taken. The meme of raids had fundamentally altered and evolved due to changing social conditions. That's not to say the original quest for lulz was entirely destroyed–plenty of chat revolved around the trope "LOL FALTERING

REGIME, let's hit it till it breaks"- but in terms of primary motivation, Lulz had been superceded by Sincerity.

The fascinating case study of Anonymous is just one example of how memes are more than a theory of information, but a concrete form in themselves. But in terms of the potential of these organisational forms, Anonymous is just an encouraging, if problematic, start. It is indicative of a changing political understanding, as highlighted by Paul Mason, in a generation entirely removed from the political landscapes of the Cold War. We will move beyond Anonymous in the coming years, as techno-logical literacy spreads beyond the geeks into the general population, and these forms become the default for young agitators and other discontents of neoliberalism, rather than the more rigid structures of old ideologies. The somewhat chaotic, rhizomatic manifestations of Anonymous politi-cal actions foreground the collapse of the concept of programmatic politi-cal movements, favouring instead a multiplicity of struggles. We are not compulsive recidivists, nostalgic for massed, unified throngs driven on by demagogues. We are more than happy to see this tactical shift, away from intrinsically authoritarian notion of "political unity", if it is to be replaced with class unity. We don't see this decentralisation of power and authority in determining the direction of actions to be a negative impact of technology. Memetics offer an opportunity for the instigation of autono-mous actions, delivering death by a thousand cuts to our enemy.

Finally we offer a very telling short anecdote, regarding the two con-tradictory drivers of memes, lulz and sincerity, that caught our attention earlier in the year. When union members and activists occupied the State Capitol in Winsconsin in an impressive defence of collective bargaining rights, it received global attention, not least because of live streaming of the occupation and a tech-savvy bunch of activists inside the Capitol. Reports started to come through of supporters worldwide ordering pizzas from the local pizzeria for those camped inside the building. Ian's Pizza's soon set up a blackboard to chart these small acts of solidarity, and they became a meme in their own right. Soon pizzas were being delivered to these North American labour activists from across the Middle East and Europe, and even China. This seemed like an important symbolic shift in the power of memes, to us. When 4chan began making raids, a staple of their arsenal was to bombard their victims with hundreds of unwanted, unpaid-for pizzas. Now, the pre-paid pizza slices arrived in their thousands, as a gesture of a shared struggle against neoliberalism. Memes have the capability to drop their amoral, malicious impetus, and become forms of political struggle, practical and moral support and solidarity. Where once Memes + Lulz = Terror, perhaps today Memes + Sincerity = Communism – or, at least, a step in the right direction.

NOTES

1   An imageboard is an internet message board predominantly used for the posting and reposting of images.

2   4chan message boards are organised alphabetically /b/ board represents the random board and is where most site traffic is driven. As a result of the nature of infantile/ offensive content posted /b/ boarders often affectionately refer to themselves and others as btards or ./b/tard.

3   The hivemind is a concept of the form of collective intelligence created when large numbers of autonomous users operate within decentralized or self-directing networks.

4   "LOL" has become one of the most popular acronyms developed for ease of communications on online and short message services (including text messaging). Originally meaning "laugh out loud", it now conveys a general sentiment of amusement or humour. In youth culture it is also used IRL – often heavily ironically. The past tense of "LOL" is "lolled".

5   Raids are carried out when the hivemind assembles to attack a single individual, government or organisation, raids usually escalate in scope rapidly and are often begun by dropping dox (finding real life addresses/names/telephone numbers of the target).

6   Part of the internal social disciplining structure within 4chan are the concept of "Fags" – "fag" connoting disapproval rather than actively implying homosexuality. These are given prefixes according to the nature of the action of which the community might disapprove – i.e. "GaiaFags", "NewFags" (newer, niave members).

7   A good example of this is the meme "in ur base killin ur doodz". The original meme was based on images from computer games where one player had infiltrated another players base and is proceeding to kill his characters (doodz). The joke was a brag. Today the image has been replaced so many times, and the slogan altered, that the original context is now irrelevant, as long as the user references the meme itself with the phrase – "in ur XXXX, XXXXin ur XXXX". If you want a taste, google image search "I'm in ur".

8   IRL= "In real life", an acronym used to differentiate between experiencing reality in fleshy first life, as opposed to reality observed through the filter of contemporary technology.

9   Internet slang for the act of posting inflammatory extraneous, or off-topic messages in an online community, such as a forum, chat room, or blog, with the primary intent of provoking readers into an emotional response or of otherwise disrupting normal on-topic discussion.

10 DDoS Attack = A Distributed Denial of Service Attack is an attack on a website carried out by flooding the host server with requests from multiple (usually tens of thousands) of users. Prior to the use of Low Orbit Iron Cannon these were previously carried out by large botnets.

11 IRC is an acronym for Internet Relay Chat, a chatroom platform developed in 1988 for group discussion, it is supported across all platforms but requires a softwareclient such as mIRC in order to participate.

If you don't let us dream, we won't let you sleep?

Ben Lear & Raph Schlembach

oint nine of Paul Mason's "Twenty Reasons" highlights the personal experience of the crisis. For many, the future looks decidedly bleaker than it has done for a long time. For us this subjective experience of the failure of the capitalist promise of unending growth and luxury underpins much of the unrest occurring across the globe. Whilst this experience changes across space – indeed some parts of the world are experiencing strong, continued growth – we see important political commonalities emerging. What connects our struggles is the rage we feel as our social wealth and dignity is attacked. These connections are not, however, unproblematic. Whilst we are connected through our hope for a better future, our task will be to ensure our hope and energy is not side-tracked into struggling for more work and less prosperity.

I. PROMISE

"Marx was right. Marx was right all along!"
– *placard on national demonstration against education cuts*

What is the "capitalist promise" whose failure is leading to our struggles? We see the capitalist promise as the political and social forms of legitimisation which capitalist development relies upon. These forms are expressed differently across space and class, from the "American dream" to Ed Miliband's "British promise" "that the next generation would always do better than the last" and the dream of export based development. The promise of capital is that of unending growth, and the redistribution or trickle down of that wealth. Tied into this promise of wealth are ideas of accessible education, social mobility, paid employment, secure jobs, freedom from debt and improvement upon previous generations. The underpinning of the capitalist promise is the belief in the ability of capital to provide social security and the means to a good life. This promise, our expectations of capital and thus the horizons of our potential futures, have been shaped by previous generations – through what was won, through what appeared possible in previous times. In Europe this is informed by the nostalgic, sepia-toned memory of the Fordist era, replete with promises of full employment, family wage and mass consumption. This isn't a case of false consciousness, of conspiracy or of capitalist "lies", but the outcome of the ways in which people invest the society they find themselves in with the hope for a better, more comfortable and enjoyable life.

This promise, as already mentioned, varies over time, across space and between different social groups. However, Paul Mason identifies the graduate without a future as a key international actor in recent struggles. Many students enroll at university in the hope of getting a better job at the end of it, a hope that is becoming increasingly unlikely as the crisis deepens and leaves large proportions of populations structurally unemployable. In North Africa and the Arab world, decades of developmental policies implemented by nationalist strongmen and autocratic monarchs have not delivered Western levels of wealth beyond a privileged elite. Those gains that have occurred are now under threat as oil and food prices rise and Western consumer spending falls. As well as being a struggle for democracy the "Arab Spring" is also a revolt against poverty, expressed in rising food prices and a lack of jobs.

What unites the experiences of student protests, labour movements and the Arab Spring, then, are their relationships to the capitalist promise. Our problem with capitalism isn't the system's "greed" or the over-consumption of seemingly "passive citizens", but the way in which wealth is produced and distributed which leads to empty homes, unused swimming pools and rusting unsold cars produced by under-paid workers living debt-financed lives. Imagining ways out of our current political and economic situation does not, and should not, entail a move towards austerity, be that enforced or voluntary. Our problem with capitalism is not that it produces an abundance of wealth but that it is incapable of fulfilling this promise for all but a privileged few.

II. BETRAYAL

Why did Nick Clegg cross the road?
Because he said he wouldn't.

– popular joke about Deputy Prime Minister

Economic crisis and enforced austerity, combined with environmental crises and rising oil and food prices appear to be challenging the capitalist promise. Here in the UK the government is using the crisis as the pretext for dramatic cuts to public spending complemented by moves towards marketisation of key public sectors; most controversially higher education and health. Economists predict that any recovery that may occur will be a jobless recovery; workplaces are being "rationalised" with many positions being permanently removed and/or being replaced with precarious, overworked temporary and contract roles. Much of the burden of this structural adjustment is being borne by young people (in April 2011, 1 in 5 of 16–25 year olds in Britain were reportedly unemployed) – trade unions are already talking of a lost generation.

Between us, the authors, having spent more than 11 years in higher education, we still have little hope of moving beyond underpaid, undervalued, under-stimulating contract work. As the university re-structures and permanent, secure work is replaced by more precarious, target-driven research we have seen our own aspirations and plans for the future dwindle away. We see many young people in a similar if not worse position than us. For those of us in the streets during the student demonstrations of the winter of 2010/11 this sense of betrayal was tangible. These were moments of convergence in which our individual feelings of betrayal found collective form. However, we believe the feeling of betrayal extends beyond those involved in the education system directly. The seeming common sense of "work hard, get a good job and live a happy life", repeated in job centres and by "lifestyle management" gurus, no longer stands up to scrutiny. For the recently unemployed, or those facing longer hours for less pay, the dream of wealth and security has been betrayed. The sense of social betrayal, of the end of the capitalist promise of wealth in return for discipline and hard work has become generalised.

Perhaps one of the best examples of how this betrayal has been expressed here in the UK is the curious rise and fall of Clegg-O-Mania. In the run up to the general election in May 2010 Nick Clegg was seen by many as a breath of fresh air and an alternative to stale party politics. After the elections Clegg became a focus of the Take Back Parliament campaign, the UK's purple movement, which sought electoral reform and had famous musician Billy Bragg as one of their strongest advocates. At one demonstration, to cheers from the crowd, Clegg explained "I've campaigned for a better, more open, more transparent, new politics, every single day of this general election campaign. I genuinely believe it is in the national interest". At this moment the Liberal Democrats were truly seen as an alternative to the self-interested, untrustworthy politics of the other two parties, an example that parliamentary politics could work.

However, by the time of the student protests and the Liberal Democrats having backtracked on their pledge to protect higher education, alongside the first wave of cuts, the situation had changed. Whilst the placards and banners still had Nick Clegg's face on them the message now read "Nick Clegg we know you, you're a fucking Tory too". Many had seen the Liberal Democrats as allies in the struggle against rising tuition fees and a buffer from the cuts and were furious at their subsequent lack of fidelity. In terms of the student struggles the Liberal Democrat betrayal convinced many people that political parties could not be trusted to defend social rights. The promise of a break with traditional party politics was betrayed brutally and "Clegging" entered the vocabulary of many, with the youth slang website urbandictionary describing it as "The process of having sold out, especially to a system or body that directly undermines the principles and values you have long adhered to". The rise and fall of Nick Clegg echoes the larger, more structural, slipping away of the capitalist promise of wealth.

The broken promise of unending growth and progress is now a reality. Although we are not "all in this together" it is a reality that cuts across many social positions, from the unemployed youth in North Africa to European students graduating with tens of thousands of pounds of debt and little hope of a job to pay it off. The crisis is being felt subjectively as a betrayal of the promise of development and growth.

III. DESPAIR
"Fuck this, I'm moving to Scotland"
– placard at student protest on Parliament Square

Nick Clegg's betrayal indicates that this is not just an economic crisis. This is also a crisis of democracy and representation. We have all experienced sentiments of despair and impotence, unable to think how we could find our voices heard. Herbert Marcuse, the great theorist of a previous generation of student protesters, wrote that the "containment of social change is perhaps the most singular achievement of advanced industrial society" (*One Dimensional Man*). We can, at times, still appreciate this feeling of one-dimensionality.

When hundreds of thousands marched "for the alternative" in London, what was this alternative that we were putting forward? Listening to those slowly making their way along Embankment, meandering into Hyde Park, we often heard arguments that begun with "of course, some cuts are necessary, but..." Current debate seems to question the speed and scale of austerity measures, not their inevitability. The TUC organisers themselves saw the day as an expression of opposition to the "fast, deep public services cuts", a demand for a more just way of administering public debt and dealing with recession, through job creation and "sustainable growth". We are trapped in a logic in which the only apparent response to crisis is the equal distribution of the burden and more work in the hope of stimulating new growth.

Outside of the political parties and segments of the institutional left we are witnessing the rise of populist politics. Unions, NGOs and social movements such as UK Uncut are calling for the implementation of redistributive policies such as increased financial regulation and higher taxation of the super rich (such as the Tobin Tax). Whilst these movements are useful in highlighting the structural inequality of capitalism, and providing a pole of attraction for angry people, we feel they fall short politically. The crisis of capital won't be stopped by recovering taxes lost to legal loopholes nor to tightening regulation.

This seeming unwillingness to imagine bigger political alternatives is contributing to the sense of despair and rage that many of us feel. The future has been made one-dimensional; all that remains is more of the same, for less reward. As long as our alternatives focus on the negotiation of wealth distribution, it is no more than a rearranging of the social condition of the present.

Our hypothesis is clear; society is capable of containing, or recuperating, our criticism and our rage. But also, and the point of Paul Mason's twenty theses is to show exactly this, there is reason to think that new possibilities are opening up that allow our criticisms to resonate further than they have before, possibly to the extent that they may rupture this one-dimensionality. These possibilities exist both within and beyond the post-political condition of the present.

The political task that we have before us is to move beyond this despair, in both its personal and collective dimensions, and re-negotiate the basis of our hope, not in capitalist development, but in its confrontation and eventual abolishment. The exciting possibilities and potentials we see within existing moments of resistance serve as inspiration and encouragement that this impossibility is a potential future yet to come.

IV. HOPE

"I thought we were going to Alton Towers"
– placard on national demonstration against education cuts

Where is the element of hope that spurs thousands into action, worldwide and across social strata?

We've been presented with a narrative of hope turned into despair; the capitalist promise of growth unfolding into a nightmare of cuts and austerity. And yet, within the one-dimensionality of capitalist existence lies hope. Hope not because of a transcendental possibility of salvation, not because of an ontological revolutionary outside, but because of a movement that grows out of the very condition of despair. Hope is not utopian, in the etymological sense of a non-place, but it is dialectical; it is already here. Capitalist accumulation entails within it the very possibility of its collapse. So we need to invert the hope-despair narrative and trace how, through our subjective experiences of crisis and despair, we emerge with new collective hopes and desires.

Our hope is also non-utopian in the sense that we are not in the business of painting detailed pictures of what a post-capitalist society will look like. That does not mean that we cannot imagine or experiment with social relationships that are not dominated by the logic of accumulation and valorisation. But it does mean that we are not concerned with the details of who will clear the rubbish off our streets in a post-capitalist society – an obsession that appears perverse in a world where millions survive only on rubbish. What we do say when we talk about an alternative is that we reject the logic of capital. The vision of a post-capitalist world is not one of paradise; we cannot imagine a world without problems and conflicts.

But we can, and must, imagine a future where the production of wealth is no longer tied to class divisions and the labour relation. Generalising this re-understanding of hope and progress as against and beyond capital is the key political task that we face.

Hope means more to us than just a defence of the present state of affairs from an onslaught of cuts and economic readjustment. We need to think about our desires not as individual aspirations to protect our lives from change, but consider seriously the possibility of controlling our collective future. Take last winter's student protests in the UK as an example. Do we really want to defend the university system as it stood before the Browne Review? We would suggest that the students demanded more than that: an education that was not tied to the market, an end to the elitism of the sector, a life of learning that was not instrumental for success on the labour market. And it was those demands that related their protests to the hopes and desires of the anarchists in Greece, the youth movements in Egypt, or the unionists in Wisconsin.

Our hope, in this sense, cannot be equated to a bourgeois pursuit of individual happiness. The possibility of a better life for all lies not simply in the demand for a more equal distribution of capitalist commodities. It lies in the recognition that capital simply cannot fulfil its promise. Ultimately, we can't be afraid to make "luxury for all" the central demand of our movement. In order to make this desire a reality, we need to recognise that "we are the alternative"; that wealth creation can be organised as a collective endeavour in which we shape our own history, where we are not the co-managers of capital, but the social movement that aims to abolish the conditions of its own enslavement.

The revenge of the remainder

Camille Barbagallo & Nicholas Beuret

Invoking memories of impoverished lawyers in Paris during the French Revolution, Paul Mason articulates his contemporary revolutionary figure: the graduate without a future.[1] This figure stalks the world stage, bringing down regimes in North Africa and spearheading resistance to "structural adjustment" and austerity in Europe. Yet a closer look at the actual life of this figure reveals it to be just one instance of life as a *remainder*. A condition endured by the mass of surplus bodies living without a future, living the general condition of being without hope that neoliberal capitalism has brought into being.

Over the last 40 years the world has seen the birth of a new kind of worker – a worker bereft of work. Workers who inhabit precarity and are deemed to be superfluous to the requirements of capital.[2] Be they the excess of educated and work-ready bodies in the world's metropolises, or the multitude of hungry and feared bodies in the slums that encircle the urban centres of the post-colonial world, these bodies are surplus to requirements – they are the remainder of capital's calculus.[3] We can trace this surplus mass of bodies, its contours and manifestations. In doing so, the act of tracing reveals something fundamental about "being surplus". The form, specifically the *body* that comes into focus is a part of the unfolding crisis in which we find ourselves, as both subject and object, its reason and its consequence.

CONTOURS AND SHADOWS...

Nearly half of the population in Britain who are aged between 18–65 are "precarious".[4] Which is to say that their work and social life is increasingly uncertain, poorly remunerated, causal and subject to sudden change.[5] They live in a world of permanent underemployment and insecurity. This precarious population includes around one third of all recent university graduates[6] and an army of working poor, including a quarter of a million workers who are paid less than the minimum wage.[7] We live in a period of increasing "necessary unemployment", characterised by the rise of the informal economy.[8] The informal economy is posited in this instance as the economic sphere beyond the formal capitalist realm. It is estimated to be worth upwards of £137 billion per year, providing employment for as many as 3.6 million people in Britain.[9]

In addition, more than being precarious, almost one quarter of the British population aged 18–65 are "economically inactive" – that is to say, excluded from waged work.[10] This figure includes the one million women who have left or been expelled from the labour market since global economic crisis began in 2008. This abandonment by capital manifests most dramatically in those classified as "NEETs" – people who are "not in education, employment or training". One in six 16–24 year olds (and almost one in five 18–24 year olds) fall into this population, which is currently one million strong and set to rise.[11] The problem is certainly not confined to Britain: within the "wealthy countries" of the G20, the last three years has seen 20 million more bodies added to the category of the unemployed.[12] This growing population who are left without work, coupled with a hidden informal workforce and the precarious bodies of graduates and the underemployed constitute the emergence of a permanent surplus population – a reminder.

The rising insecurity and precarity of life is also apparent in the new forms of poverty that have emerged in Britain as capital and the state try to explain that they can no longer afford us all. Five million households live in "fuel poverty", unable to afford heating, "water poverty" affects four million households[13] and a new "food divide" defines who can eat what, with dramatic implications for their health.[14]

Beyond the ever more militarised borders of Europe lies a world increasingly determined by the growing volume of surplus bodies and by the battle to contain them. Over 1 billion people now dwell in the world's slums and the number is likely to grow to 2 billion by 2030.[15] The informal economy accounts for the economic activity of almost three quarters of the world's workforce outside of the centres of wealth accumulation (and also for 15 percent within them). In addition to this space of the economically marginalised, the global unemployed now number over 200 million, with many more not officially counted. Ultimately, we can trace the shape of this surplus life in the sheer mass of the hungry. There are 930 million malnourished bodies throughout the world, not for lack of food but for lack of money: there exists enough food to feed them all one and a half times over.

Even though it is radically differentiated depending on where in the world the body is found, beyond the sheer volume of surplus bodies there exists a simple and common relation – of waged work to survival. Which is to say that the millions of bodies who are the surplus population need the wage to survive, but they lack sufficient work, or sufficient guarantees of work. As a result their lives sit precariously balanced between life and death.

TOO MANY, TOO MUCH

Start from the beginning. Each year, year after year, fewer workers produce more commodities as labour becomes more productive. Productivity is a curve, arching towards the sky, cumulatively reducing the number of workers needed for any one process or workplace. A simple example: last year ten workers were needed to produce one shoe. This year only eight. And so it goes, on and on. Hence, if capital stands still, if it fails to continue to expand there emerges a problem, one of a shrinking number of workers/consumers, and a growing mass of unsold commodities and unutilised capital. Accordingly, year after year, the number of workplaces, markets and consumers must grow. Grow or die – such is capital's imperative.[16] If capital doesn't expand, the unsold, unused and unemployed will only grow while waiting for an eventual crisis to sweep it all away in an orgy of destruction. So more – more factories, more commodities, more markets – must be created. But it is also workers who are dependent on capitalist expansion in the form of more jobs. If capital stands still it not only produces a growing mass of unsold commodities and unutilised capital but also a shrinking number of jobs. As labour increases its productivity it makes itself redundant, and can only find more work in new industries, factories or territories. If it can't, then it is free to starve. For the workers of capitalism are those bodies who have been "freed" from any other means of subsistence than the wage.

Let's come at it again. Capital needs bodies to work, to produce and ultimately to consume. It can only encounter those bodies if there exist bodies who *need* to work and *must* buy in order to consume. Until relatively recent times, the vast majority of the world's population produced, under different regimes, enough to subsist. They did not need to go out to seek a wage to buy the means of their own reproduction. The process of creating capital's workers is the bloody process of destroying other means of life: appropriating or destroying the means of reproduction outside of the wage relation.[17] The enclosure of communal lands and the destruction of indigenous civilizations had to occur and must continue to occur in order for capital to grow and therefore survive. It must destroy those rights that exist in opposition to the only rights recognised by capital: the right to work, the right to starve and the right to choose between them. The ongoing process of dispossession creates workers simply because, dispossessed, they must work for a wage to survive. It also creates a steady stream of wealth (be it gold or oil; fish or knowledge) that fuels the fires of accumulation. This dispossession sows the seeds of capital's growth. Capital chases itself around the globe, destroying other ways of life in new territories, opening up the possibility of new markets in which to sell commodities where once there was subsistence, and in doing so reaps the harvest of capital beyond the limits of existing markets.

This expansion takes place not just in space but also in time. Here debt enters into the calculus, as a mechanism that allows capital to move between the future and the present. Debt provides the means by which workers can buy today what they will earn tomorrow. Just as capital seeks to harvest new territories, debt enables a harvesting of the future. But, at some point, the books must balance and the debt must be paid or *look as though* it will be paid. The present must return in the future as more of the same. It is the balancing of the books that drives the system into crisis. For while a frontier exists – more bodies, resources and territory and so a balance of forces can be maintained through on one hand, growth and expansion and on the other, ever more productivity. But without an outside to incorporate, an outside that continues to exist, it is impossible to keep the books balanced.[18] Because no growth means no new markets and also no new investment opportunities, jobs or avenues of development. Without a frontier, capital ends up exhausting the possibilities of the spaces it already inhabits, eventually entering into crisis.

It is precisely this moment of impossibility that we have arrived at, and not for the first time.[19]

RETURN TO THE START

An ever-growing mass of surplus bodies find themselves starving amidst plenty, while capital runs out of profitable avenues of investment. Mountains of debt pile up next to unused machinery and unsold products while workers are unable to find work, piling misery upon misery as all kinds of poverty abound and grow. What was this moment's genesis? Forged in a series of trends, tendencies and circumstance, the current situation we find ourselves in was brought into being when a threshold was crossed in 2006 with the subprime debt crisis in the USA.

This tipping point was produced by three factors. First, a greater global demand for the raw materials of production and consumption combined with a reduced supply of them increased the basic cost of living in the USA (though, to be sure not only there). Second, massive inflows of speculative capital into a range of different markets, most importantly into those that "managed" housing mortgages (especially the so-called "subprime" mortgages) and basic commodity markets, looking for returns free from the fetters of decreasingly profitable material production (again increasing the cost of living and the cost of doing business). Third, a greater reliance on the market by the world's population with the reduction of non-market mechanisms of reproduction (such as the welfare state or exchange, barter and subsistence). All three of these factors led to a squeeze on incomes – waged and unwaged – to create a surge in the cost of living.[20] This led directly to the collapse of the ability of the USA working class to pay its debts, especially that section of the working class that were always precariously balanced on the edge of poverty. This collapse, coupled with volatile and deregulated international markets, set off a chain reaction of panic and uncertainty as to the actual "worth" of the pile of debts, derivatives, futures and other arcane financial instruments in the world's financial markets that has yet to completely play itself out.

A growing world population reliant on markets for their every need hit a limit: only so much raw material, only so many factories and refineries, so much oil, food, water, etc. can be created. There is only so much world to put to work. It was certainly not a lack of bodies but a lack of materials for those bodies to work with that started to drive up prices, especially of food and basic commodities. The massive increase in the hungry, homeless and poor in the lead up to and through the crisis speaks to the successful destruction of economies outside of capitalism. To be sure, feedback mechanisms such as climate change, desertification and pollution all helped squeeze the "environmental supply". Financial speculation played its part too. But it is ultimately the combination of the need for growth and the lack of life outside of capitalism that caused so much hunger. This lack of raw materials also hints at the reasons for the explosion of speculative and financial activity.

Ours is a world running out of profitable avenues for investment, one in which speculation reveals itself as the only place left to generate profit. The future is mortgaged, but payment is always eventually due. And this payment plan is one that requires bodies to work, to consume, to create debts and ultimately to pay when the bill is due. This mortgaging of the future ran ahead of itself, got too far beyond what would ever be earned or could ever be paid. Without the space to expand, or the consumers to spend, there was no hope of loans being honoured.

The spark that lit the fires in the streets was both the neoliberal assault on the future prospects of a large part of the population in the world's wealthy countries and the further impoverishment of the precarious and surplus bodies of the world. It was the combined effects of too much capital, too many workers and not enough new frontiers for expansion that caused a shortage of raw materials and the means of reproducing life. It is this spark that connects Somali pirates, driven to piracy by the destruction of their fisheries, to the food riots around the globe in 2008, to the revolutions in North Africa, to the demands for higher wages in China, to the riots in Britain and across much of Europe. This crisis – a crisis of the very relationship between labour and capital – signals the reaching of limits, of processes that have come to their terminus and given birth to the figures of the *remainder* we see stalking the world stage today – which includes the graduate without a future to be sure, but also the surplus population that dwells at the margins that are quickly becoming the centre of our world.

A QUESTION OF CONTROL

At the edge, bereft of frontiers for expansion or opportunities to invest and with a decline in the need for labour, the question that haunts capital is no longer how to put bodies to work, but how to control and contain those bodies excessive to the work available. For us, workers without wages or security of income, the question is no longer seizing the means of production – production as it stands only renders us superfluous and undermines life itself. For us the question is how do we once again reproduce ourselves beyond the wage. This world of control is characterised by the rising importance of a politics of abandonment and containment, which according to Achille Mmembe can be conceived of as "necropolitics" – where death and not life is the function of governance.[21]

With a surplus population, managing death is the core concern of political activity. One of the key political tasks is allowing them to die without endangering the section of the social body that must remain productive. Surplus humanity – the bodies dwelling in slums, ghettos, refugee camps, prisons, old people's homes, remand centres, disaster zones like New Orleans and Fukushima[22] and of course all those existing in the informal economy that are beyond any utility for capital – it is these bodies that are abandoned at as little cost as possible. This is necropolitics: the politics of containment and abandonment in a world without resources beyond the market.

This practice of allowing people to "fall behind" operates through a range of practices and discourses centred on a kind of Darwinian racism: a purity of ideas perfectly matched to the rhetoric of neoliberalism and the "right to be unequal" held so dear. Necropolitics operates through diffused institutions – private companies, aid and disaster relief bodies, personal militias and government agencies. It creates a series of fragmented territories that disable mobility – territories in both the physical (slums, estates and prisons) and social sense (as in the idea of hoodies or welfare cheats).

Walled off and policed, these territories are maintained separately from those spaces deemed productive. Through a permanent state of siege the borders are maintained by either postcolonial policing (racial profiling, stop and search powers, ASBOs, anti-gang activities etc.), economic exclusion (such as redlining, or lack of educational facilities) or ideological public campaigns of shame and stigmatisation (against the unemployed, the migrant, the diseased or disabled). For all the differences that exist between exclusion through ASBOs *vs* containment via migration regimes or precarious service industry work *vs* informal micro-credit debt, the underlying logic is the same: contain, fragment, isolate and abandon.

Kept apart as less than fully human, as not able to contribute, as a threat and contagion, these bodies are then allowed to die. Slowly. Inch by inch. Through hunger, ill health, disaster, gang violence, poverty and disease. This is the fate outlined by capital for one third of humanity today.

REVENGE

Contrary to the story of disaster relief operations, just wars and those that would put "more cops on the streets", this crisis cannot be solved through legitimate means; justice will not prevail. A balance of forces cannot be struck because there is a limit to justice. The limits to justice are ultimately configured by what it is: an ethical practice, grounded in the exercise of some *legitimate* authority, aimed at restoring a balance, or business as usual. But what sort of justice can be entertained today when the processes at work either destines us to a life abandoned, awaiting a meaningless death, or balanced precariously on the edge? There can be no hope of bringing back some kind of Keynesian social pact, nor should we want one. For it was built on the unwaged and devalued labour of women, the underwaged labour of bodies in the colonies, not to mention the existence of an environmental abundance of resources that no longer exists. No, there is no going back, nor is there any kind of deal that can be struck. Justice is not possible.

Only revenge is possible. By revenge we mean the inflicting of wounds so grave that our enemy suffers more than we do. A hatred of capital is necessary, but a rage to injure and inflict revenge from below is also required. Yet alongside this necessary violence, a process of salvage is needed. At this juncture, the question must no longer be one of better terms within a system that will only confine us to an ever-worsening condition, but one of escape. An armed escape. We must return to the fundamental question of life beyond the wage. We must seize the means of reproduction, violently, and with a hatred of a life enslaved.

NOTES

1   http://www.bbc.co.uk/blogs/newsnight/paulmason/2011/02/twenty_reasons_why_its_kicking.html.

2   However, contrary to Mason's argument, organised labour remains a force actively resisting the rule of neoliberal capitalism. Many of the recent revolts, from the occupation of Tory Party headquarters at Millbank in 2010, to Tahrir Square and the worldwide #occupy movements in 2011, intimately involved union organisation

and the labour movement. In *Forces of Labor: Workers' Movements and Globalization Since 1870* (Cambridge: Cambridge University Press: 2003), Beverley Silver argues that the proportionally dwindling formal labour workforce is still organising and is still a force to be reckoned with. See for the example of truckers in China: http://www.wsws.org/articles/2011/apr2011/pers-a30.shtml.

3   There have been an increasing body of work that addresses the concept of a surplus humanity, including Mike Davis, *Planet of Slums* (London: Verso, 2006), Achille Mmembe, "Necropolitics", *Public Culture* 15 (1): 11–40, *Rethinking Capitalist Development: Primitive Accumulation, Governmentality and Post-Colonial Capitalism*, ed. Kalyan Sanyal (New Delhi: Routledge, 2007), Michael Denning, "Wageless Life", *New Left Review* 66, November–December 2010, and *Endnotes*, 2, "Misery and the Value Form". In his notion of "the second contradiction of capital", James O'Connor develops the idea of the necessity of an abundance of bodies outside of the formal capitalist economy in connection with the concept of an environmental surplus.

4   http://precariousunderstanding.blogsome.com/2007/01/05/precarious-precarization-precariat/.

5   This destabilization of life where there was once security under the welfare or developmental state is not simply a return to an earlier epoch of capitalism; or, rather, it is both a return and a departure, as we will see. It is the development of a mode of life far from past avenues of escape (to new towns, workplaces, frontiers or colonies) or non-capitalist modes of subsistence (from communal land to familial relations). This lack of open space and other means of life, as well as a massive increase in environmental degradation and transformation, mark this situation as one different to past periods of generalised insecurity. See 13 below.

6   http://www.telegraph.co.uk/news/uknews/2656219/One-third-of-graduates-do-not-benefit-from-having-a-degree-report-says.html.

7   http://www.statistics.gov.uk/cci/nugget.asp?id=591.

8   International Labour Organisation, http://www.ilo.org/infeco.

9   http://www.futurematters.org.uk/drivers/informaleconomy.asp.

10   http://www.statistics.gov.uk/cci/nugget.asp?id=12.

11   http://www.guardian.co.uk/education/2011/feb/24/young-people-neets-record-high.

12   "Report warns of deepening global jobs crisis", http://www.wsws.org/articles/2011/sep2011/jobs-s28.shtml.

13   http://www.guardian.co.uk/environment/2011/feb/20/water-poverty-uk-scarcity-bills.

14   http://news.bbc.co.uk/2/hi/business/4652801.stm.

15   Davis, *Planet of Slums*.

16   David Harvey, *Limits to Capital* (London: Verso, 2007).

17   Karl Marx, *Capital* (Harmondsworth: Penguin, 1976), Silvia Federici, *Caliban and the Witch* (New York: Autonomedia, 2004), *Midnight Notes* 10, "The New Enclosures" (1990), Harvey, *Limits to Capital*.

18   One of the most significant and valuable "outside" spaces that is produced and maintained by the capitalist mode of production is the domestic household. It is in this space that the unpaid work that reproduces life (work that is still overwhelming performed by women) is captured by capital in a process mediated through commodity production – in particular, the commodity of labour-power – see Mariarosa

Dalla Costa and Selma James, *The Power of Women and the Subversion of Community* (Bristol: Falling Wall Press, 1975).

19   It's important to note that a surplus humanity has come into being in pervious epochs. The creation of a surplus humanity is both a cyclical and secular process – that is, it continually reoccurs, but reoccurs in ever-greater numbers and proportions. It comes into being when the limits of an existing world-system are reached (the physical limits, for expansion and reinvestment as well as with regards to resources), so that whatever space constitutes the limits of a system that cannot, for that moment, be expanded, are completely consumed, obliterating all non-capitalist space, making further grow impossible.

20   Commodity prices started to creep up in price in 2003, then took off just prior to the sub-prime crisis in 2006, resulting in a food crisis in 2007/8 and again now in 2011, as well as fuel and other basic living cost crisis around the globe.

21   Achille Mmembe, "Necropolitics".

22   On disaster zones as areas governed by necropolitics see Silvia Federici and George Caffentzis, "Must We Rebuild Their Anthill? A Letter to/for Japanese Comrades" (http://libcom.org/library/must-we-rebuild-their-anthill-letter-tofor-japanese-comrades), and Rebecca Solnit, *A Paradise Built in Hell: The Extraordinary Communities That Arise in Disaster* (New York: Viking, 2009).

Fear and loathing

David Robertshaw, Rohan Orton & Will Barker

C an young radicals pick and choose their battles or take a day off? In the case of Egypt for example, dissidents find themselves in a position where the consequences of retreat would be costly despite cosmetic changes at the top since the uprisings in February they remain exposed and vulnerable – the Egyptian state has continued to crack down on protesters in Tahrir Square, bloggers have been locked up for criticising the military, a state of emergency has been called and protests have been banned until September. Allegations of torture are abound, amongst others those of female protesters being forced to undergo "virginity tests". The notion of radicals being able to take a day off quickly appears to be a eurocentric one in the face of this evidence.

The British, as a case in point, operate in a completely different context to the Egyptians. Although the police and ACPO[1] have been capable of many dubious actions from a civil liberties point of view, they come nowhere close to the widespread abuses of the Egyptian military. The Egyptian and the British protester do not face the same consequences if they choose to confront the state. It follows then that fears of different types of repression are counterbalanced by different demands. As our social contexts and compositions differ, so too our fears change. In Egypt, a large number of people are experiencing abject poverty when faced with the rising cost of living and when they take on the state they are risking their lives. In Western Europe, we don't worry about being disappeared by the military but we are frustrated by the absence of meaningful control over our lives.

Raoul Vaneigem made a distinction between life and survival, asking whether we want "a world in which the guarantee that we shall not die of starvation entails the risk of dying of boredom."[2] With this in mind, it is not so much a matter of losing fear as one set of fears outweighing another. If the thought of continuing to live in this world of mere survival becomes more terrifying than the threat of arrest, then inaction becomes more terrifying than a night in the cells or a black mark on your work record. Fear is a matter of losses weighed against gains, and if we are to look at what British society offers we can see how little we really have to lose.

We speak as people in our twenties and thirties, and our situation seems to be different to that of our parents' generation. Where the post-war generation saw increases in job stability, with stronger rights in the workplace and the establishment of a welfare state, ours has seen a decline into precariousness. Today there are few who have any illusion about having a job for life and even fewer who will attain such a thing. There has been a massive reduction in permanent employment, with an emphasis placed on greater mobility and temporary contracts. This move towards short-term and temporary employment has been accompanied by a reduction in workers' sick pay, holidays and other rights. It can also be seen as a major cause of the stagnation or reduction of wages for most people in this country for the past 30 years.[3] Another factor that draws heavily into this feeling of precariousness is the explosion of debt: credit cards, mortgages and student loans have the effect of trapping people into a greater dependence on working harder, working longer hours and forgoing the niceties of regulation.[4] Precariousness does not just exist in the realm of work (the disappearance of stable jobs), but can also be seen in housing, welfare provision, levels of debt and other areas of our lives.[5]

In the current economic climate, many graduates have been unable to find highly paid work, or any work at all. Studying at university as a solid investment in a stable career is becoming a difficult idea to reconcile with reality. Many young middle class graduates with good qualifications are finding themselves signing on, stacking supermarket shelves, doing low skilled casual and temp work. It is difficult for those who do succeed to ignore the fact that many of their course mates are being left behind. Middle class parents are confronted with the fact that their children or their friends' children are unable to find work. Not only are their children incapable of finding work but their own jobs no longer feel as secure as they once did. Slashes to public spending have resulted in mass redundancies and have brought this sense of precariousness to the door of middle class white-collar workers. Even among the relatively privileged, the awareness is increasing that the current system is failing them.

This awareness brings with it a sense of fear that pulls people in two directions. On the one hand towards increased atomisation – a sense that others pose competition to them. This creates tensions between groups. Fear finds itself redirected to resentment and malice levelled against all too familiar scapegoats: migrants, travellers, so-called "work shy", or "the greedy unions". On the other hand, what offers more hope is that this fear is also driving people to group together and take collective action, becoming political and forgeing solidarities. Recently, we have seen this manifest itself in various forms, e.g. occupations of universities and marches against government cuts.

Changes in the stability of work have also had effects on the forms that struggle takes. The old working-class based movements of a generation ago have by and large disappeared. The forms of organisation that accompanied them have similarly faded away, with industrial action increasingly viewed as a tool for the self-interested worker rather than a manifestation of class solidarity. Today it would be hard to conceive of strikes as the main form of mass action, union membership has declined and the power of unions has waned since the 1980s.[6] In part this is due to the legal limitations that have been placed upon the unions, including the ban on flying pickets. However, it is also the time commitments necessary for participation in unions that often appear as an insurmountable hurdle. Time is scarce for those working long hours to pay off debt or keep their jobs and houses, as well as maintain their families. Raising one's head above the parapet by getting involved in workplace disputes is more and more daunting to those who can so easily be cast aside by their employers. Moreover, it is simply not an option for the temp worker, illegalised worker, or for the unemployed, because unions have little power or interest in fighting for rights on their behalf.

The workforce has become increasingly mobile, passing easily not only through a variety of companies but also through different sectors: one month doing secretarial work for the NHS, another selling insurance over the phone. Due to this, workers have a vested interest in the struggles of employees in a wide number of sectors because they have been or know that they may at some point be employed in that line of work.

This same increase in movement means that people feel less loyal to their jobs, employers and bosses. This makes it easier to rebel, because they have fewer emotional ties to their employer. The bosses are abstract entities, disconnected from the individual's sense of identity. Moreover, it is possible that this reduces the animosity that people feel towards management for whom they are only able to muster a vague sense of resentment.

Yet, just as mobility creates more of a distance between workers and employers, it can also result in workers experiencing a similar distance between each other. Precariousness in the workplace can mean a diffusion of social solidarity that stems from a collective identity. Co-workers come and go rapidly, and the mass association of the factory floor has given way to the atomised teams of the call centre; commitments to each other are hard to establish. The long hours people spend at work, the increasing death of public space and the greater geographical mobility of populations, all cause problems for the creation of geographical and working communities. There are no local working communities any longer.

It is not a new thought that the internet has been instrumental in creating new communities based on shared interests and common difficulties, from manga enthusiasts to haemophiliacs. These online associations are of great importance because they change how information is disseminated and how links can be made. As topics spread through Facebook and Twitter, they provide access to much wider varieties of people than would ever be possible via geographical or labour associations. At the same time as advances in communication affect what is politically possible, they also alter how people interact with politics. Communities are no longer distinct entities, identifiable by the physical spaces that they occupy. A single internet forum may consist of several intermingling communities, spreading out into Instant Messaging, Facebook, Twitter and various blogs. Identifying who exactly belongs to the community becomes impossible, which means that questions of how and whether a community will act are entirely unpredictable.

When resistance escapes the confines of the internet and moves from sharing information to acting on it, there comes a tipping point where retreat is no longer a practical option. Yet the fluidity of our relation to the online world does promote an attitude of picking battles wisely. Blogs are regularly abandoned or forums closed without much fuss. Their creators and commentators disperse, keeping some of the connections made and losing others. New communities are created elsewhere; indeed, the participants probably have a slew of others anyway, sitting in their bookmarks. This happens so regularly that organisation becomes perceived as something transient, a constant process of death and rebirth as congregations change to meet changing needs. A recent example of this would be the purging of political Facebook groups just before the Royal Wedding.[7]

One constant remains in all this fluidity. Although some commentators will always have their opinions more highly regarded than others, people are frequently left with the general idea that their opinions matter. In order to belong to web-based communities it is not possible to be passive. To be inactive is to say nothing and if someone only lurks they are invisible to the community, they occupy no space there. Disagreement with or expansion on the words of others becomes the easiest way to belong. It promotes an environment that is the antithesis to traditional political structures, where the directives of the hierarchy are not to be questioned and the job of the masses is to follow where they are led. So, becoming a pawn for rigid, dogmatic organisations becomes harder to accept. The very processes involved in online communication push us towards ways of thinking that go against being directed as a mere member of the rank and file, there to fight and die as directed.

All this makes for an environment in which people can participate to a greater or lesser extent, where participation is not as straight forward as turning up to a picket. The "front lines" of days gone by only exist on rare occasions, instead we have a situation where engagement cannot easily be measured in such physical terms. Our increasing connectivity means that struggle has become a constant aspect of our lives, even if it may not always appear so to the outside observer. Yet, we must remain vigilant to some of the dangers that lie before us, as it could well become all too easy to slide into the least confrontational forms of action and remain there; precariousness might mean we have less to lose, but what we do have is so much easier to lose. The fear remains.

NOTES

1   The Association of Chief Police Officers (ACPO) has recently been the subject of controversy after the identity of one of their undercover operatives, Mark Kennedy, was

discovered. The media uproar following revelations of Kennedy's activities prompted the removal of ACPO's control of their three "domestic terrorism" teams. Travis A, Lewis P & Wainwright M, "Clean-up of covert policing ordered after Mark Kennedy revelations" *The Guardian*, January 18th, 2011: http://www.guardian.co.uk/uk/2011/jan/18/covert-policing-cleanup-acpo.

2   Vaneigem R. *The Revolution of Everyday Life* (London: Rebel Press, 2003), 18

3   Harvey D. (2010) *The Enigma of Capital – And the Crises of Capitalism* (London: Profile Books, 2010), 12.

4   For up to date information and statistics on UK personal debt, a good source is the Credit Action website http://www.creditaction.org.uk/helpful-resources/debt-statistics.html.

5   It is important to note that precariousness is not a new phenomenon, it is the rule to which the post-war generations' ability to find secure work and have strong rights is the exception: throughout the history of capitalism this has been the situation that the working classes have found themselves.

6   Figures charting the decline of the unions can be found in the Department of Business, Innovation and Skills publication, *Trade Union Membership 2010* http://stats.bis.gov.uk/UKSA/tu/TUM2010.pdf.

7   Malik S., "Activists Claim Purge of Facebook Pages" *The Guardian*, April 29th, 2011: http://www.guardian.co.uk/uk/2011/apr/29/facebook-activist-pages-purged

A funny thing happened on the way to the square

Thoughts in the middle of the Athenian autumn of 2011

Antonis Vradis

S omebody asks: how do your days pass in Athens? I find this a difficult question. First, because I cannot even estimate whether I spend most of my days in the Greek capital, as I am near-constantly displaced between Athens, London and elsewhere. But second – and this is more complicated – because it feels as if something strange has happened to our understanding of time in the past few years. The revolt of December 2008 was a spectacular crack in the path we used to tread. It was as if everything until then culminated in a single point in time – and that our reality has since hung mid-air; days trail endlessly and blend into one: an entire society entering and then remaining in limbo.

But this limbo is not a pause, not at all. On the contrary; from the moment when Alexis dropped to the ground, hit by a police bullet on that Saturday night in Exarcheia, the rusty wheels of history have gone into delirious spinning. Until a few years ago, most of us would have not expected to ever witness the series of events that have since been unfolding before our eyes: the 2008 revolt; the strike-back of the state and its normality in its counter-insurrection operation that followed; the IMF/EU/ECB agreement and the misery it entailed for so many, so fast.

I think back to the crazy euphoria of the summer of 2004, the last and highest moment in which the capitalist spectacle exposed itself on Greek territory. The spectacle created and enforced singularities before sweeping them all under its veil: the complete alienation of capital. When the spectacle was at its peak, any meaningful ties of solidarity – of community – hit an unprecedented low. It could only have happened this way.

Then I fast-forward to the summer of 2011, shell-shock in the face of IMF/EU/ECB agreements slowly giving way to all of their repercussions. During this summer, Athens had an eerily unfamiliar vibrancy. A few years earlier, summer was a lethargic time for the city: locals drifting en-mass to the closest family house or to a cheap resort; tourists replacing them, overflowing the Greek capital to trace its ancient past before embarking to the nearest island. That was how it was some years ago, a quiet time. But the current times are far from quiet. This summer, thousands flocked to Athens' main square, Syntagma, night after night, their chants cutting through the breeze-less Athenian summer nights. People who had never taken to the streets before met each other, held daily popular assemblies at the square, discussed into the early hours, organised themselves on the ground and prepared for what quickly became a full stand-off with the government: a square, a city, a people in spectacular turmoil.

I want to try to comprehend what the changes that brought these people out in public mean, not in terms of how we *do* politics, but how we *make* politics – how we create new understandings of what is political, understandings that encompass more than we had conceived to be the political sphere. To do away with the idea of representation, i.e. some abstractly-understood power, to not allow allowing decisions to be made far away from us with little or no space for us to influence their outcome. Paul Mason's point on contemporary political actors having the ability (essentially, the luxury) to *"take a day off"* was a great trigger. For me, this point raises questions not so much about the luxury to choose when to fight, but about the connection to and the relevance of each of these fragmented, limited struggles for our lives and the lives of others.

In the past years, there has been a dramatic change to the way that we conceptualise these struggles. But before delving into these changes, some background on the Greek context is necessary.

WHAT YOU CALL MODERN, WE CALL "NEVER BEEN"

A hopeful aspect of the Greek December of 2008, the square occupations of 2011 and the thread of struggles linking the two, has been the relative absence of a fixed political discourse. This, after all, is a country with a fierce political history, a social setting that carries the scars of fierce battles over quintessentially political matters: another, not-quite-invisible, thread exists linking a civil war, a dictatorship and a succeeding democratic regime within and against which so many struggles have been fought. Not quite the continuation of politics by other means; wars in the past century in this Southern European land have been nearly as continuous and constant as politics itself.

As explained by Giovanopoulos (2009) Greece, or rather, the Greek economy, never fully underwent a complete industrialisation process. Greece never saw the factory chimneys smoking over the mountains of its mainland or its islands as were seen in the English North, the American Rust Belt, or the Italian Northern Industrial Triangle. Industrialisation started late and was interrupted early, thanks to the global shift of production east of North America and Europe. And so, this never-completed process saw Greek society make a leap from a pre-industrial to a post-industrial one, largely omitting the in-between. Bruno Latour (1993) famously said "we have never been modern" – perhaps a label Greeks could use too.

In the political terrain, this has translated into the formation of political agents that have not been explicitly nor firmly linked with their workplace. This is not to say that there have been no significant workplace struggles here – on the contrary! – but that social and political struggles have followed quite a different trajectory. They have followed a trajectory that understands each individual as less of a singular identity (a worker) and more as an augmentation of identities (a worker, a family member, a member of a specific ethnic group, etc.). This might explain why political consciousness seems to be running relatively high around here, much boosted by this augmentation of identities, combined with a rich history of political tension and struggle. And yet of course, in the years of the seemingly endless euphoria, the reduction of the consciousness of individuals to nothing but passive consumers was near-absolute here too. In struggling for whatever right you were struggling for, you would not only have been forgiven for taking a day off, but even somewhat expected to do so and to cease being publicly involved once that struggle was over. You would be expected to take *all* days off any broader, political engagement. But after December 2008, things could not stay the same. The state of emergency declared on the side of state resonated on the side of those struggling – something changed, for good.

WHATEVER HAPPENED TO THE DAYS OF TAKING A DAY OFF?

One of the most formidable weapons that power has at its disposal in order to enforce its rule is compartmentalisation. The British Empire divided in order to rule over its subjects. But this division need not only run between populations – the line can run pretty much through any-where, especially between an individual's different life functions. For Giorgio Agamben (2000) this is a prerequisite for state sovereignty, as it "can affirm itself only by separating in every context naked life from its form" (2000: 11). But there is something deeply ironic here. The Greek state (and in this it is not alone) is turning fast into what Agamben called the "spectacular-democratic state", "the final stage in the evolution of the state-form – the ruinous stage toward which monarchies and republics, tyrannies and democracies, racist regimes and progressive regimes are all rushing" (2000: 86).

There are two distinct parallel processes taking place here. On the one hand, the state is converging toward its absolute spectacle, this "ruinous stage" where national borders begin to matter little, where ideologies of the mainstream political spectrum are rendered increasingly irrelevant. Of course Greek territory is a fine example: it no longer matters what fraction of the unified parliamentary party is in power, and it is starting to matter less whether parliament exists at all.

While this convergence is happening (this implosion of political ide-ologies and modes of governance all coming into one), there is a simulta-neous explosion – a forced attempt to rule through division, through the absolute fragmentation of people's life, social, and political functions. In other words, the idea that single-issue activism can be effective, or that during struggle (or afterwards) it could be possible or even necessary to take a day off; even worse, to have a day of struggle before going back to normal (think of the dozens of anger-diffusing general strikes called by the government-friendly trade unions in Greece)

But what happens when there is nowhere to take the day off *to* – or when one struggle becomes inextricably connected to another, then another, then another? Activists can pick up social struggles, take time off and shift between them only for as long as social tension remains rel-atively controllable, when the "wrongs" can be identified in a larger sea of "rights". There is a tipping point, however, where the causes to fight for become a major issue in one's own everyday reality, when there is simply no escape, no way to go back home. Just like in Tahrir Square and in Puerto del Sol, something funny happened to the people congregating at Syntagma, day after day, night after night. What brought people out there was anger. But what made them stay put, what empowered them to break away from the convention of leaving once the ritualistic demonstration of their discontent had been showcased, was a different matter altogether: in the gigantic assemblies, in the endless discussions lasting late into the night, a new realisation started to sink in. A realisation that this struggle was much bigger than any single demand or any mere attempt to slightly re-figure the plexus of power. Against an all-out capitalist assault, any meaningful response could only be as complete, as all-encompassing as the assault itself. If there was to be any meaningful change, there would be no more separation of struggles – every single struggle is my own. And there would be no more time to take off – every moment is a moment of struggle. Somewhere on their way back to the square, disgruntled citizens and specialised activists would become revolutionary actors.

GOOD THINGS COME TO THOSE WHO JUST WON'T WAIT

Somebody asks: how do your days pass in Athens? I try to explain. They protest: "but doesn't this become a struggle for its own sake? An endlessly monotonic tempo? No matter what happens, your answer is the same: fight. And then, when do you have the time to think, to produce, to love, to live...? Just being active is not being productive. Shouting slogans, always the same slogans, will never inscribe anything firm into the ground."

The idea of *"hav[ing] a day off' from protesting, occupying"* (#13 in "20 Reasons") is similar. On the one hand, an idea that the demise of organised working-class movements brings a type of revolutionary flexibility that essentially works to our movement's advantage. But on the other hand, this presupposes an understanding of occupying as an intermission between renting; of protesting as being separate from living. Giorgio Agamben wrote the text quoted earlier in the chapter in his critique to our understanding of ourselves as "citizens" who demand "rights" from the state – a veil covering the absolute control of power, through the illusion that it is possible to demand and to score victories before returning to so-called normality. And yet, one of the most stunning things about the struggles of the past years in the Greek territory is that people's understanding of their enemy has shifted from a specific class or single economic issues toward and understanding of their enemy as an all-encompassing power. The slogans of the short-lived Syntagma Square Occupation movement were too vague to be realisable without the radical overthrowing of the existing order as a whole. We saw the firmness and determination of the thousands who stayed put in the face of a police onslaught on the square this summer – and then we saw them returning to the square, assault after assault, before spreading the spirit of the square occupation into neighbourhoods, workplaces and their everyday life. As it is the capitalist onslaught that takes their days away, taking a day off their struggles becomes a non-option. All facets of social resistance have swiftly merged into one, and their days seem to blend into one. These are extended moments of struggle to take back all of their days – to take back their entire lives.

REFERENCES

Giorgio Agamben, *Means Without Ends* (Minneapolis: University of Minnesota Press, 2000)

Christos Giovanopoulos, *December and the City* (unpublished article: 2009).

Bruno Latour, *We Have Never Been Modern* (Boston, MA: Harvard University Press: 1993).

Antonis Vradis is a member of the anarchist collective Occupied London, a PhD candidate at the Department of Geography, LSE and the *Alternatives* editor of the journal CITY. He is a regular contributor to the blog *From the Greek Streets* (http://www.occupiedlondon.org/blog) and co-editor, with Dimitris Dalakoglou, of *Revolt and Crisis in Greece: Between a Present Yet to Pass and a Future Still to Come* (Oakland and Athens: AK Press and Occupied London, 2011).

The revolution is my boyfriend

Tabitha Bast & Hannah Mcclure

"**T**he revolution is my boyfriend!", declares Gudron, the parodied archetypal protest leader in Bruce LaBruce's 2004 film *Raspberry Reich*. And it is her we think of, not a real woman like Asmaa Mahfouz who "sparked the Arab Spring" or Commandante Ramona of the Zapatistas: from the opening scenes of her haranguing her boyfriend to fuck "out of the bedroom, onto the streets!", her constant monotone sloganeering about the sixth generation Red Army Faction, as ludicrous as "cornflakes are counter-revolutionary", to the scene where she orders two men in her group into homosexuality for the revolution. Gudron is indeed leader, organiser, facilitator and spokesperson. Undeniably, when finally she declares the Revolution postponed it feels as if it is her place to do so.

We laugh with both sympathy and recognition. This is a woman we know from history, from films, from our own experiences. This is the full time activist, the educated young woman who populates struggles now and always. This is not a direct comparison to the woman we see today – we're not saying the two are the same. Gudron's archetype aids us in an inquiry into the way our relation to movement is born out of the production of images, slogans and compositions – but also expressed through the roles we play and how we relate to struggle. With a commitment and passion like the most intense of romances, the revolution is indeed her boyfriend – as it has been ours.

We are familiar with this role, this passion and this intensity for revolution. But what role, if any, did this female archetype of an educated woman with a lust for change have in the recent wave of struggle? We are aware that the explosive and viral character of the past year of struggle has undoubtedly generated transformative images and political interactions. Analysing the composition of the struggles we discover young, precarious workers, intellectuals, school children and graduates taking to the streets. This wave broke through more than geographical borders as town after city after country after continent became infested with this passion. Amongst the many visual and textual accounts littering both social and professional media were striking images and words of the women within these struggles. Photo after photo of women in Middle Eastern and North African countries facing down lines of riot police or marching in hijabs with fists raised in the air.[1] The second is of the prominence of women in Europe protest movements, be it women on microphones in Plazas across Spain, or of girls linking arms around a police van to protect it from the rage of youth.

Differences in access to education and labour markets, different cultural norms and gender roles will be reflected in different roles women play in these distinct struggles. While recognising differences, contradictions and complexities within the multitude of movements that formed this year's uprisings we are focusing on – broadly – the Arab Spring and the (mostly) student dominated movement in the UK. We are particularly interested in – and have attempted to weave this narrative throughout the chapter – the way the overt involvement of women links with some of the other "reasons" Paul Mason refers to: the educated person with no future, the increase in social media, etc. This interweaving of "reasons" is not because the question of the role of women has no weight on its own, but rather, as can be seen by the striking headline of an opposition paper, women stand with multiple guises:

> She is the Muslim, the mother, the soldier, the protester, the journalist, the volunteer, the citizen.

With this we share an understanding that, unlike our Gudron, us real women do not have a singular identity. Nor are our identities constructed in isolation from those of the men we struggle against and alongside.

Our investigation into the statement draws us not to answers, but to more questions. If the Revolution is My Boyfriend, then the Revolution is Not Me. It is not just children that women take care of, but their lovers too. This caring, supportive role may provide the backbone of a movement, but it is not the same as taking part in leadership, where we still see women excluded from leadership and spokesperson roles. This echoes the role the majority of women play in a capitalist market, where women take on the function of reproducing capital by being heavily involved in the upkeep of labour-power, as primary care givers for both the family and services industries, which both help to reproduce and keep capital productive. Women as workers will of course play a key role in struggle, this is because women form the core of informal and reproductive labour which is under attack from the many neoliberal encroachments taking place around the world.

These roles are paralleled in the crucial and indispensable responsibilities women often have in protest movements today. For example reports from the Arab Spring state that,

> Women were involved in arranging food deliveries, blankets, the stage and medical help... They treated the injured in the streets and nursed them in their homes when they were too afraid to go to hospital.[2]

However, we also recognise that within the social dynamics of the current struggles there is the blurring of boundaries between leadership and the backbone. What is exciting about this resurgence in movement is not woman leading instead of the man, but rather the lack of key spokespersons, key media organiser and the disintegration of the need for the "archetypal" protest leader as we know it. This is politics with a face of many. We are witnessing a more collective and generalised rage against the structures and relations of our everyday lives and the mistrust of those in power. This has created an outburst in extra-parliamentary forms of struggle going beyond the need for traditional political leadership. Again, we do not wish to fetishize horizontal organisation, but we accept that it provides a potential for change and flux in places it has not already and ironically become institutionalised.

Our second question is around *who*? Who is this backbone woman? Who is this female "archetypal protest leader?" Young, educated women are numerous in the current wave of struggle but they have always been! Firstly, women have always been the pin-ups for social movements. From the masked and armed women in guerrilla armies across the Global South, to the young female suicide bombers of Palestine, to the poster that turned many of us onto politics as teens, that of Vivian during the Poll Tax Riots going for a cop with a pole. These images of rebellious, and often beautiful women, provide perfect propaganda for the Left. Far from the claims that women have gone unnoticed, it seems these portraits of women in struggle have dominated the imagery from movements even though women have made up the minorities in street protests. If the Revolution is My Boyfriend, we want to look good on his arm.

According to estimates, "at least 20%" of the crowds that thronged Tahrir Square in the first week were women.[3] But "at least 20%" seems low when considering other struggles. For example, In the Liberation Tigers of Tamil Eelam (the "Tamil Tigers") women were active in up to 40% of the group's suicide attacks and this level of participation is common amongst Kurdish and Syrian terror groups.[4] Likewise, within the UK, women have been heavily involved in the direct action movements from the 1970s through to the 1990s, sometimes in dominant numbers and often with more than "backbone" roles. This is also true of more recent direct action groups across the UK. If the numbers and roles of women have meaning, perhaps we can detect some here: through the UK environmental and anticapitalist movements, women taking the role as facilitator, organiser and full time activist together with an explicitly feminist politics perhaps changes the structure of how we organise. This can make those involved question privilege and male-dominated spaces, and start implementing structures that allow for greater and more inclusive involvement.

Ah, but let us return to the educated young woman! As explored previously, educated young women have often inhabited a role within movements that is not definitive of woman in her different stages of life. Before the relatively likely (though of course nation-, race- and class-dependent) event of Motherhood, women's position is entirely different both within our political circles and in our most personal of relationships. Both education and youth place women in a unique position amongst their less privileged sisters, who are far more numerous than the educated young woman who often represents womankind on the front-line.

The role for older women meanwhile often remains that of Mother, even within our social movements. Mothers protecting their sons or their husbands through demonstrations, anger and tears. This is not to downgrade the role of Mother but rather to illustrate the limitations that face women within social movements. Facing down traditional roles to create new ways of being is somewhat more of a project than facing a line of riot police.

As Sina Gabil vocalises,

> People have been conditioned intellectually, psychologically and religiously to discriminate against women. To change this will be a lot harder than getting rid of Mubarak.[5]

Recognising the limitations women face and the role youth, education and class play within our social movements, we would also like to ask the question, *so what?* If women are numerous in social movements is this a process of struggle creating "gender equality", new forms of relating outside the confines of token state policies changing? Women's interests within social movements are different, and often contradictory. For example, the middle-class women within the Arab Spring have been focusing their political energies on issues of political representation and on laws affecting women's equality. The working-class women are typically more concerned with wages and workers' rights.[6] There are shared struggles against violence and for voice, but the expression and demand may conflict within women's class interests. We are again wryly sympathetic to Gudron when she declares: "All roles alienate equally but some are more despicable than others."

It is imperative to analyse exactly what the function of women is within social movements. Using traditional limitations and stereotypes of women's role has been credited with inspiring much of the Arab Spring when women appealed for their menfolk to take to the streets. We urge caution with how triumphantly we should see these apparent subversions. Working within the constant dynamic of power while we subvert the meanings imposed upon us to rise up, the cooption of women's role as peacemakers, negotiators and carers will be continually used against the potential of the movement.

It is interesting to reflect on that image of the girls surrounding a police van that had journalists panting during the student uprisings in the UK. What were those girls doing? And what were the media doing who paid homage to the women as the correct and upstanding representation of manageable protest? Zoe Williams, the much-exalted demonstrator who protected property from rioters – and not just any old property but the police van, a symbol of state power – became the hero of the *Daily Mail* and its like, which noted with, one imagines, little critique:

> The teenager, a first-year History of Art student at the Courtauld Institute of Art, previously attended the £12,500-a-year Colfe's School in south-east London where she left with four A grades at A-level.[7]

She seems perfect for the role of educated, young woman who exemplifies the social movements, rather than her streetwise working-class counterparts who were kicking in the windows.

What then can we conclude? Our truthful answer is: nothing. We can only ask more questions and that questioning must not end. To believe in conclusions is to believe in utopias. We watch and act keenly though, to see if our voices go beyond the need for political representation and an equality based on neoliberal market-based rights. We suggest that women as workers – as students, as mothers – as our many different productive roles we claim, and use to relate to one another, need to question how we relate to one another and recognise how we, in our daily lives and struggle, both challenge and confirm the status quo. We can challenge by recognising our role as reproducers and workers, as part of a wider collectivity and struggle, but can confirm by slipping into identity politics, biological determinism and fear. Underlying these questions regarding limitations, equality, roles and struggle, the Madrid-based *Precarias a la Deriva* collective argues that,

> capital fragments the social in order to extract value, we join together in order to elevate it and displace it toward other places.[8]

Women are indeed numerous and are dynamic, exciting and crucial parts of the recent uprisings spanning across the globe – but as workers, as women, as revolutionaries, we need to question and eradicate a value system based on competition and economic productivity so that collectively we can figure out and fight for what we truly desire.

Without participating in struggle, women's lives will not be changed. But the way we participate and the way we represent our participation in these struggles is constantly in tension between changing and colluding with dominant ideologies . With rebel joy we take to the streets but it is as much in the transformation of the occupiers as the occupation that we rejoice. We have faith in the power of action, but only when coupled with critical thought. Indeed, this is one marriage we wish to uphold. It is not enough to be the girlfriend of the Revolution. If this is all we get, we sincerely declare the Revolution Postponed.

NOTES

1   http://muftah.org/?p=928 , Dotsen – Renta, L, "Revolutionary Women: Mirroring Latin America & The Arab World"

2   http://www.guardian.co.uk/world/2011/apr/22/women-arab-spring , Rice et al, "Women have emerged as key players in the Arab spring"

3   http://www.thenation.com/article/160179/arab-spring-women , Cole, Juan and Shahin "An Arab Spring for Women"

4   Dugdale-Pointon, TDP., Suicide Attacks – Terrorist, http://www.historyofwar.org/articles/weapons_suicide.html.

5   http://www.worldcrunch.com/arab-spring-female-factor/2999, I, Mandraud, "Arab Spring: The Female Factor"

6   http://www.thenation.com/article/160179/arab-spring-women , Cole, Juan and Shahin "An Arab Spring for Women"

7   http://www.dailymail.co.uk/news/article-1332811/TUITION-FEES-PROTEST-Students-streets-girls-leading-charge.html#ixzz1SjcJ8J4m , R, Camber et al, "Tuition Fees Protest: Britain's Students Take to the streets again – this time women are leading the charge."

8   http://zinelibrary.info/files/A%20Very%20Careful%20Strike.pdf, The Precarias a la Deriva, "The Silent Strike"

Do the entrepreneuriat dream of electric sheep?

Why contemporary activists talk about power

Andre Pusey & Bertie Russell

It is perhaps an exaggeration to suggest, as Paul Mason has, that those blockading either Tahrir or Parliament square are well versed in their Hardt & Negri, much less their Deleuze, Guattari or Foucault. Yet it doesn't take a bookworm to realise that the forms of struggle witnessed over the past six months surpass any simplistic "us and them" binary, and that a more nuanced understanding of power is required if we are to come to terms with the battles we are fighting.

The authors Mason refers to are, in our opinion, indispensable in helping us understand the shifting arrangements of power and its relation to the changing forms of capitalist accumulation. Things seem significantly different now for a variety of reasons, with recent uprisings in Tunisia, Egypt and Libya among others, as well as an upsurge in struggle in the UK and across Europe – things seem to have started to *move*.

Despite claims to novelty or "newness", to a greater or lesser extent, all of the authors Mason mentions belong to the Marxist tradition, albeit in a bastard form. Marx's "old mole" – the movement which abolishes the present state of things – has not gone away, but has just been lying low, experimenting with new concepts, drawing from the commonwealth of different intellectual traditions and struggles. Far from substituting a critique of "class" with "power" *per se*, as Paul Mason has suggested, they instead suggest that *different forms* of class struggle are needed – forms that spill beyond the factory walls and political parties to take account of the diffuse methods by which capital "accumulates our souls" in contemporary society. In this chapter we wish to outline some of the ways we think capital and class composition have been transformed. They are tentative ideas and suggestions, to be developed further.

1.   The late 1960s and 1970s saw the beginning of a substantial shift in the technical composition of class. In what is commonly referred to as the shift from "Fordist" to "post-Fordist" production, what began to be abandoned was the organising of production *en masse*, where thousands of workers were mapped out on factory floors by a handful of "foremen" that operated as mini-dictators. These mini-dictators commanded everything within their factory-kingdoms; where workers stood, how long they stood there for, what their hands did, how fast their hands moved, and so on. The social composition of this Fordist production model hence appeared to imitate a form of sovereign power, which is to say, the foreman appeared to directly organise and direct the space, time and bodies that fell under their command.

2.   The shift from a Fordist to a post-Fordist organisation of production did not so much abandon these forms of disciplinary workplaces that relied on the foreman-dictator, rather they displaced their prominence. Not only were these actual Fordist sites of production shifted geographically to the global South and East, but this *form* of organising production was displaced by new regimes of production based on novel forms of control. In other words, new forms of organising the process of production emerged in certain "developed" areas of the world that increasingly did not rely on the foreman-dictator to enforce our compliance, but rather the emergence of the manager-magician.

3.   Unlike the foreman-dictator, the manager doesn't directly discipline the worker through informing what tasks must be undertaken, how they are to be performed, and in which order they must be performed. The foreman-dictator operates using mechanical or analog forms of power, where a worker is considered to be an inert lump of flesh and bones that must be directly animated if they are to perform any "useful" task. Under the auspices of the manager, the workers are interpreted as autonomous subjects that are permanently electrified. The "magic" of the manager is that she can make things happen without apparently forcing anything directly. So where the foreman-dictator had to use force and overt coercion, the manager uses more subtle forms of power, getting things to move as if by "magic". Given that these electrified-workers are already active, conscious, living beings, the task of the manager-magician is not to force them to

move like a wooden puppet, but to create the "fields of sense" within which these electrified-workers then operate of their own accord. The electrified-worker doesn't perform a task because a foreman dictates what to do; she performs multiple tasks without specific instruction, having been put on a *general trajectory* by the manager-magician. We are no longer in motion because we are being directly animated by the foreman-dictator; we are in motion because it "makes sense" to perform certain tasks according to the logic set out by our managers. We are no longer being shoved with a wooden stick but animated within digital fields of sense, at times accompanied by jolts from electric shocks, although it is increasingly difficult to identify their origin.

4. The electrified-worker, rather than an inert vegetal mass put into motion by the foreman-dictator, now appears as a self-motivated and dynamic "entrepreneur". The worker is no longer primarily valued according to the extent to which she can be efficiently disciplined and have time extracted from her. Instead, the valued worker is one who has learned how to "use her initiative", who is capable of "thinking outside the box", and who can constantly invest (without dictation) in her own capacity to be a flexible, efficient, and dynamic entrepreneur. The old axiom "socialism equals soviets plus electricity" turns out to be the tagline for the Facebook generation.

5. This new *entrepreneuriat* operates increasingly without any punch-card to register when they are or are not working; this form of measurement and method of delineating work and play belongs to the Fordist organisation of production. As the development of the social factory expanded the field of capitalist production and value extraction across society, time itself became saturated by capital. The entrepreneuriat is never on or off, but permanently electrified and permanently in motion. As the Italian "autonomous" Marxist Franco 'Bifo' Beradi has suggested, "Capital no longer recruits people, it buys packets of time [...] de-personalised time is now the real agent of the process of valorisation, and de-personalised time has no rights". In this sense, we find that we are living in a state of precarity, where despite the fact we find ourselves permanently investing in ourselves, we increasingly work on fixed-term contracts or without a contract altogether.

6. Rather than appearing as an homogenous group to be disciplined by the foreman-dictator, the individuals of the entrepreneuriat are self-motivated to constantly assess, measure, and invest in themselves, with the purpose of becoming more "dynamic" individuals. Rather than begrudgingly undertaking "industrial training" at the behest of the foreman-dictator, a state of permanent education is demanded, actively pursued and increasingly funded by the entrepreneuriat itself. The entrepreneuriat desires constant investment in *Me Inc.* to raise their personal stock of *human capital*, ensuring that it can perform better in the market competition between workers.

7.   As the entrepreneuriat, we increasingly interpret our co-workers not as comrades united in mutual exploitation under the dictates of the foreman-dictator, but as "healthy" competitors. We don't stand united as a class in the face of capital, we run against each other in the name of self-improvement. There exists only a modicum of solidarity with fellow co-workers. Of course we care for them and share our coffee breaks, but we are ultimately aware that we are in competition with them. Who can sell the most Levi 501s in the next four hours? Who can secure the longest phone contract? Who can publish the most articles, or guarantee the return custom? The investment in *Me Inc.* is no longer just in customer service training or getting a degree, but in whitening your teeth, enlarging your breasts and getting hair follicles implanted/removed. The body itself has become an investment opportunity.

8.   The most successful corporations are harnessing competition and putting it to work, so that electrified workers compete against each other *in the name of improving the health of their collective body*. We are put to work against each other and we don't even realise it – instead we buy into a myth that this competition is for the "collective good", and that those that are not-up-to-scratch will have to be amputated for the good of the collective. We are close to the wildest of perversions where the amputated entrepreneuriat supports and understands its own redundancy – "for the good of the body".

9.   If the post-Fordist transition saw a move from the foreman-dictator to the manager-magician, we have increasingly seen the latter transform into our comrades, offering us "pastoral care" and complimentary *Me Inc.* investment guidance to "help" us deal with the anxiety of full-spectral-competition. We are increasingly operating as self-managed autonomous entities, investing our own temporal, psychological and financial resources into our own training. The foreman-dictator is increasingly becoming superfluous; his analog, mechanical techniques are no longer effective, as there is no longer an inert vegetal mass that requires directing. The good "manager" is now more of a carer and a "friend", someone who helps you "fulfil your potential" in your competitive endeavour against others. Perhaps the most developed example of this exists within the university system, where managers are increasingly cast as "pastoral" carers, whilst weekly emails offer you "opportunities" to enhance your individual ability to engage with industry, deliver presentations effectively, write successful grant bids or increase your "networking" skills.

10. The manager-magician has ultimately become the new *therapist*, attempting to help the worker constantly adjust to a world that is moving increasingly too fast to comprehend. This form of therapy can be understood as the psycho-social restructuring of our fields of sense in the interests of capital. The way we understand ourselves and those around us, the way we interpret and act upon the world, is constantly being refined to ensure our emotional compatibility with capital – therapy in the name of "normalising" ourselves, or to overcome the anxiety, panic and depression that results from operating in a world in which we don't fit.

We need to abandon forms of therapy (and forms of thought) that suggest that it is *us* that is the problem, and instead construct militant therapeutic practices that enable us to collectively recognise and break with those "fields of sense" that limit our lives and capacities. The therapy we need to engage in is based on collective action and analysis, so that we can learn to create our own – common – "fields of sense".

To be explicit: we are not saying that the entirety of the class is now organised this way. Rather, we are drawing attention to the increasing prevalence of the new "social technologies" through which we are governed (and govern) in the interests of capital. Nonetheless, it is clear that as these technologies proliferate, the forms of resistance that assume power still operate primarily according to the logic of foreman-dictators disciplining our bodies, will be increasingly ineffective. Capital began to abandon such forms of sovereign direction when we found ways to effectively resist it in the 1960s and 1970s. One only has to look at the impotence of recent strike actions and traditional trade unions to see that revolutionary techniques can no longer be found in any "overthrowing of the boss". Instead, we must, out of necessity, forge techniques of collective resistance that operate not against someone or something "out there", but against ourselves – against the entrepreneuriat and the digital value systems that organise our desires.

This is a process of exodus, via the exorcism of generalised self-investment in ourselves! This exodus is not a territorial flight, but a desertion of the role and values developed as the entrepreneuriat. Of course, the working class has always been a diabolical category; the purpose has always been to abolish our role as workers, defined as such by our subsumption under capitalist command.

Some in the anti-cuts movement see the increased social antagonisms developing within society, anger over the rich evading tax, cuts to social services and increasing fees, and wish to bring back to central stage a certain preordained version of an alternative – an orthodox Marxist-Leninist crystal ball that can inform us that "one last push" will abolish the present and give birth to a Socialist future. However, we don't subscribe to this idealist conception of how history moves – nobody is willing to give away the ability to write their own futures anymore. The problem we face, however, is that we don't yet know how to be "in organisation" in a way that will precisely allow us to move in, against and beyond capitalism. What appears almost certain is that this will necessitate a co-ordinated psycho-social deprogramming – a sort of collective social therapeutic process to extricate ourselves from the new forms of control that capital developed whilst we were still dreaming of cutting off the king's head.

Radicalising the armed forces

Federico Campagna

In the beginning, it was the navy. On the morning of October 30th, 1918, the sailors of the battleship Kiel mutinied, forcing their commander to flee under cover of disguise. In the following days, more and more German battleships were taken over by their sailors, who, together with workers from the cities, created councils for direct democratic decision-making. The unrest quickly moved to factory workers and to the rest of the army, to the point that, on November 9th, 1918, the socialist leader Philipp Scheidemann proclaimed the onset of revolution, an action which finally led to the end of the war and of the Kaiser.

Today, in the winter of 2011, which reminds some of the "spring of nations" of 1848, it is once again the army that plays a crucial role in the success of popular revolts across North Africa. In Tunisia and Egypt, mass demonstrations found solidarity in large sectors of the military, which did not oppose the popular insurgency and even helped to bring down the regime. In Libya, the initial armed confrontation against mercenary troops hired by Gaddafi was made possible by the defection of the police and their active and military support of the protest movement.

The American theorist and anarchist Noam Chomsky once said that engaging in armed confrontation with the State is a suicide attempt, as "if you come with a rifle, they will come back with a tank, if you come with a tank, they will come back with a fighter jet". At a first consideration, such a statement seems to be irrefutable. The State, in most parts of the world, does not only have the monopoly on the use of "legitimate" violence, but also has exclusive access to all possible means of a military confrontation with external or internal enemies. However, it is indeed in Chomsky's sentence that is hidden the key of a possible breakthrough. Specifically in the word "they". Who are "they"? It might seem that "they" refers to the State and its powers. Nonetheless, this is not an accurate interpretation. "They" are the army and the police, that is, the effective, practical holders of all the means of military action. In fact, Chomsky's sentence holds a deep truth, one that may escape his initial intentions: it is "them" who have the power to decide on the result of any imaginable social unrest.

Seen with the eyes of the democratic West, and in particular with those of people on the left, the army and the police seem to belong to a dimension of existence that has very little to share with that of the civil population. After the end of mandatory conscription in most European countries, the military has increasingly become a highly specialised, elite force that resembles more the armies of private contractors than the popular armies of the past. Like the caste of warriors of some ancient civilisations, most armed forces of the West have lost any real contact with the lives and desires of those populations that they supposed to defend. Furthermore, just like in those castes, the level of democracy internal to the armed forces has now reached the all-time-low of a tight hierarchical organisation.

Today, after decades of devoted pacifism, it is difficult for most of the European left to remember the positive role that large sectors of the army played in several moments of revolutionary struggle. Also, and more strangely, to remember the experiences of radical politics that often took place within old-style, conscripted armies. We could mention, for example, the Italian groups *Proletari in Divisa* (Proletarians in Uniform) in the 1960s and the 1970s. During those years, Italian society witnessed an amazing level of social tension, with the radicalisation of the class conflict and the self-mobilisation of large sectors of the population belonging to far-left organisations. The young people entering the army at that time brought into the barracks that same revolutionary spirit that was shaking other disciplinary institutions such as factories, prisons and schools. The aim of *Proletari in Divisa* was that of challenging the hierarchical structure of the army, as well as its obedience to the interests of the government and of the ruling class, and that of supporting and connecting with the social struggles happening all over the country. Despite the clear illegality of it, on several occasions thousands of radical soldiers marched in their uniforms, their faces covered by red scarves, alongside workers and students.

Soldiers also called for strikes inside the barracks in solidarity with strikes happening in the factories, started their own democratic councils and even issued their own publications.

Of course, this seems to be a universe away from today's experience of what British nationalists call "our boys" deployed as occupation troops in Afghanistan and Iraq. However, it might be the case that such a dramatic change in the role and the potential of the army for progressive, revolutionary social change has to be blamed in part on the *a priori* pacifism of most sectors of the left. Apart from the occasional, often shallow, reminder that "policemen are the sons of workers", there have been virtually no attempts in recent years to explore the possibility of transforming the armed forces from an element of governmental repression and subjugation to one of popular liberation.

Today, as much as in the past, most people in the army and in the police come from working-class and underprivileged backgrounds. In some cases, such as that of the UK, they lack of the most basic rights as workers. Since the Police Act of 1919, for example, British policemen and women have been denied the right to strike and even the right to join trade unions, which have been substituted by a government-run organisation, the Police Federation of England and Wales. Moreover, in recent years the British government has significantly eroded the right to conscientious objection by police officers – which is guaranteed by a warrant from the Crown that allows each officer to act as an individual at their own discretion (therefore, they cannot be ordered to arrest someone if they believe that not to be the right course of action) – by employing non-warranted Police Community Support Officers.

However, this is not enough to stop the armed forces from becoming arguably the strongest accomplices of State and corporate domination over national and foreign populations. To say it in Marxist terms, the fact that most of the armed forces are in "in themselves" part of the proletariat, does not imply that they are part of the proletariat as a revolutionary class "for itself". Examples such as that of *Proletari in Divisa* and of countless other experiences before that, though, show that this is not an impossible shift to make.

It is in the best interest of the radical social movements that are now springing up everywhere across Europe to imagine how this could happen. Maybe, instead of aiming at engaging in often pointless confrontations with the police, movement participants could make an effort to meet policemen and soldiers out of their working hours and engage in friendly, informal, subtle moments of direct propaganda. They could try and understand what are the tensions and injustices internal to the armed forces and support the privates in their claims for a decent and equal treatment. They could invite them to political meetings, introduce them to their friends and turn institutional enemies into personal friends.

This kind of strategy could achieve a number of important results. First of all, it would give these workers, employed in an authoritarian structure, the possibility to reclaim their basic rights, both as workers and as human beings, and to perceive themselves as less separated from the civilian members of the community they live in. As French psychoanalyst Jacques Lacan pointed out, the essence of perversion is the feeling of irresponsibility for one's own actions. In this sense, the politicisation of workers in the armed forces, who are institutionally encouraged to embrace perversion in return for immunity, and their integration within the civilian community would discourage this psychotic separation, which is at the basis of most police abuses.

Secondly, it would be a gracious twist of irony, as it would mirror the common police practice of infiltrating radical political groups. Despite all possible effort to politicise soldiers and police officers, the very structure of the armed forces will always be deeply embedded within a wider system of economic and social power, privileges and inequalities, of which they are the designated guardians. Thus, the institutions that compose the armed forces are still to be considered and treated as natural enemies. In this sense, it would be advisable for radical movements to create their own system of intelligence and their networks of infiltrators within the armed forces, in order to gather information and possibly to prevent their strategies of repression.

And finally, but most important, there is no more effective way to disarm a person than to disarm his or her brain. And, which is maybe more important, there is no better way to gain access to military strength, if necessary, than to gain access to the brains that control it.

Federico Campagna, born in 1984, is an Italian writer and activist, based in London. He writes on radical politics and political philosophy, with special attention to anarchism. He is a member of the online multilingual platform Through Europe (http://th-rough. eu). He is a regular contributor to the Italian magazines *Loop* and *Alfabeta2*.

Some complications
...and their political economy

Emma Dowling

> little men from elite society
> telling us to build a big society
> take the pin–striped suits and show them the door
> then cut the rich, not the poor.
>
> *– Captain Ska*

What of the responses by the state and capital to the current circulation of struggles? Whither these most recent movements of movement? These seem to be the questions on Paul Mason's mind as he offers us "some complications" to his twenty theses – theses he qualifies are generalisations that require further investigation, reflection and refinement to which the collection of essays in this volume are a contribution. In these caveats, he reminds us of the methods the state has available to it to co-opt or repress and therefore avert struggles for social transformation. Whether this is through infiltration or through a mimicry that aims at subverting and thus weakening movements, or whether this is through outright repression and scare tactics: cyber-attacks and restrictions to internet access, pre-emptive surveillance and arrests, as well as violence against the disobedient bodies that continue to occupy streets and squares. Mason also reminds us not to fetishise forms of organisation and communication as ends in and of themselves. Networked, virtual forms of communication and organisation do not "belong" to resistance or to progressive movements; the state and capital are as immersed in the current networked forms of communication and organisation as much as social networks and virtual communications have been conduits for the most recent uprisings; the question is one of power.

Mason ends on what he observes as the persistence of a disconnect between people and governments: the state's inability to legitimise the politics of austerity. That is, the massive transferral of wealth from labour to capital, ever-more precarisation and the further subsumption of society under capital's enclosure and exploitation are processes that not only require positively couched discourses of legitimacy, necessity and common interest to engender consent, but are processes that demand of the state the enforcement of obedience through control, as well as the repression and criminalisation of dissent. In the UK, the Government is currently trying to deal with three facets of crisis. Firstly, there is the need to legitimise the cuts in response to protests that have reached deep into the social fabric. Secondly, there is the need to create the conditions for the reproduction of labour power in the face of an intensified crisis of social reproduction precipitated upon the restructurings that have been unleashed. Thirdly – and this is crucial – there is a need to find drivers of economic growth. During the crisis of the 1980s under Thatcher, the Conservative mantra was that there was no such thing as society. This time around, the Tories are propagating at least what on the surface of it seems to be the opposite: an intense belief in the importance of the social and the need to harness its potential.

The buzzword of the Conservative Party's 2010 election campaign and since then, of the Coalition Government's austerity measures, has been the "Big Society". Encapsulated in the Big Society is the intention of drastically cutting government funding to public services and to charities, voluntary organisations and social enterprises whilst – using discourses of "empowerment" and devolution – encouraging a culture of community engagement and social activism as investment opportunities for corporations and banks. As Paul Mason observes, in the corridors of Westminster bigging up society is serious business. The Big Society is intended to alleviate the three main headaches the UK Government has, namely legitimation, social reproduction and economic growth. Let's look at each of these in turn.

LEGITIMATION

On the level of legitimation, the Coalition Government and Big Society ideologues such as Nat Wei, Phillip Blond, Jesse Norman or venture capitalist Sir Ronald Cohen have not yet been very successful. The "Big Society" is emblematic of the disconnect that Paul Mason highlights: for the Government the "Big Society" is the solution, yet it seems that for everyone else, the Big Society is ridiculed as a big joke. Political commentator Polly Toynbee has branded the Big Society a "big lie", trade union leaders have called it a "smokescreen for the cuts" and the direct action network UK Uncut have organised "Big Society bail-ins" against the UK Government's bail-outs, occupying banks to protest the cuts to welfare state. The voluntary sector is also not happy: here the argument prevails that it is precisely the cuts that will stall not promote a Big Society, with Labour Party leader Ed Milliband fuelling this for his party's own ends.

In any society that is premised upon the privileged appropriation of socially produced wealth – aka capitalism – the problem for the state acting in the interests of the privileged – aka capital – is how to justify the inequitable distribution of the social surplus. The problem only intensifies with austerity in which these transfers of wealth in the direction of the rich become much more apparent. But, legitimation is not just about what politicians say in their speeches and press releases, and our task is not simply to unearth the true ongoings behind their "lies". Legitimation is also about the material concessions that the privileged are forced to make depending upon the power relations that exist in society. Often, power relations are such that no or very few concessions have to made, and many times politicians are not necessarily lying. The Big Society is an example of this. It's important to recognise that the Big Society is not just vacuous propaganda on the level of discourse dreamt up by Conservative Party spin doctors and fellow travellers. What matters – literally in that it has materiality – is that the Big Society is the attempt to use the state to reorganise society for its further neoliberalisation. The only lie that is being espoused is that these restructurings are equally in everyone's interest. Whilst vociferously rejecting any claims that "we are all in this together", dissing the Big Society and what stands behind its rhetoric is certainly appropriate, we shrug the Big Society off with a suppressed laugh at our peril. The cuts do not undermine the Big Society, the cuts *are* the Big Society and we are not just being goaded into its affective dimensions, we are being forced into it by the political and economic restructurings that are taking place.

CRISIS OF SOCIAL REPRODUCTION

In order to maintain a degree of social cohesion, the state has to legitimise the cuts and the imposition of the commodity form on ever-more areas of social life. However, to maintain at least a minimum level of stability for capital accumulation, the state also has to address the worsening crisis of social reproduction and the need to reproduce labour power to maintain the system of capital accumulation, because labour is the key source of value for capital. We need not view the reproduction of our labour power as simply consumption – going to the shops and buying what we need and want (and can afford). Nor is it simply the ability to access public services such as health care or education. The reproduction of labour power also involves huge amounts of both waged and unwaged work, work that we do. For capital, the source of social surplus is unwaged labour, therefore, as feminists have pointed out with the example of housework, if it is made invisible and not counted as work, it can be more easily controlled and manipulated and it does not have to be paid for. Reproductive labour is often made invisible as labour, precisely in order for it be valorised by capital without capital having to afford the cost of this labour, or in order to keep the cost of this labour as low as possible. The Big Society then is about increasing that huge amount of work that we do in its unwaged form, i.e. for free. Using the affectively enticing discourses of mutualism, cooperation, collectivity and empowerment, the state off-loads the cost of the crisis directly onto us all. As we are already all well aware, the banks have and continue to be bailed out and public services cut such that they are no longer available for us to access (unless we pay for them individually at the point of delivery). But, perhaps even more poignantly, by appealing to notions of community – i.e. to all of us to provide services in the name of caring directly for one another as opposed to asking the state to do so – the Government is drastically reducing the social wage and making us work more for less and in many cases, for free. The rhetoric of care, compassion and community is an attempt to make work not appear as work so that it does not have to be negotiated as such and remunerated. Thus, the concern with social cohesion is not only a concern with averting protest and resistance, it is also a concern with the crisis of social reproduction that is being dealt with by off-loading the cost of the reproduction of labour power – and of life – directly on to the individual worker and away from the state (and capital). The bind that we find ourselves in is that the work of reproducing our livelihoods is work that has to be done and work that we care about doing – childcare or eldercare being two of the most obvious examples – it is not work that can easily be refused or stopped via a strike.

HARNESSING SOCIAL ENERGIES FOR ECONOMIC GROWTH

In the same way that the state's response to demands for wages for housework by feminists in the 1970s was to enable the capitalist marketisation of the household, the Big Society is not just spitting us all out from the state and letting us get on with self-organising our lives and self-managing the common (aside from the obvious question of who is going to have the time, energy and resources to do even more work without being paid for it). Instead, what is happening is that the neoliberal project that New Labour already embarked on with its support for the development of the social enterprise, Public-Private Partnerships and Private Finance Initiatives, is undergoing a shock doctrine style speed up. Here, the Conservative ideological obsession with the lean state meets the need to find drivers for economic growth – capital's solution to the crisis. The Big Society in this respect is the desire to harness the energies of the social to create new markets for financial investment and capitalist valorisation.

The easiest and quickest way to understand this is to follow the money. The Big Society of course cannot rely on compassionate free labour alone, it needs resources. The resources will be provided primarily by the Big Society Bank, funded by four of the major banks (Barclays, Lloyds, HSBC and RBS). In order for investment to make good business sense for a bank, it needs to receive returns on its investment. A few of the questions that as yet remain unanswered are, what interest rates will the banks charge for the loans and investments they make? To what extent will shareholders be involved in decision-making? It is not difficult to envisage that the logic of investment banking – even when it is social investment banking – will be to pressure Big Society projects to make organisational decisions that make "good business sense", i.e. that provide financial returns on investment. Furthermore, what are the criteria with which the state assesses and gives out contracts for service provision by organisations competing for contracts and for money? Who will govern the Big Society, will it be venture capitalists or will it be us? And will it deliver on its ideological promise of all-round happiness? The answer is to be found in the rhetoric of the question.

The social investment market is supposed to grow. Rendering social energies productive for capital goes hand in hand with the deregulation of existing markets (such as education, health and housing) to pave the way for a truly corporate Britain in which everyone is enmeshed. The ethical appeals that are so central to the ideology of the Big Society are interestingly spun as being commensurate not only with care, love and compassion as opposed to greed, individualism and selfishness, but also with forms of social organisation that were previously associated with the Left, such as employee-ownership, mutuals and cooperatives. These forms are being made compatible with the values and language of competition and entrepreneurism. The disconnect in the values and language of the state and those of young people that Paul Mason identifies is one that the Big Society is supposed to close by positing false dichotomies of "good" versus "bad" human behaviour, of virtues versus vices, of caring versus being selfish, of communities versus individuals – coming down firmly on the side of the former in each case. Their vision is a kind of depoliticised ethical technocracy run by virtuous experts with the help of all of us. What is the political economy of the complications Paul Mason leaves us with at the end of his article? It is our solidarity and creativity in and against the Big Society, the antagonism of our livelihoods versus capital's incessant search for valorisation, and the role of the state in the struggle to impose those conditions that make that valorisation possible.

APPENDIX Twenty reasons why it's kicking off everywhere

Paul Mason

We've had revolution in Tunisia, Egypt's Mubarak is teetering; in Yemen, Jordan and Syria suddenly protests have appeared. In Ireland young techno-savvy professionals are agitating for a "Second Republic"; in France the youth from banlieues battled police on the streets to defend the retirement rights of 60-year olds; in Greece striking and rioting have become a national pastime. And in Britain we've had riots and student occupations that changed the political mood.

What's going on? What's the wider social dynamic?

My editors yesterday asked me put some bullet points down for a discussion on the programme that then didn't happen but I am throwing them into the mix here, on the basis of various conversations with academics who study this and also the participants themselves.

At the heart of it all are young people, obviously; students; westernised; secularised. They use social media – as the mainstream media has now woken up to – but this obsession with reporting "they use twitter" is missing the point of what they use it for.

In so far as there are common threads to be found in these different situation, here's 20 things I have spotted:

1.   At the heart if it all is a new sociological type: the graduate with no future

2.   ...with access to social media, such as Facebook, Twitter and eg Yfrog so they can express themselves in a variety of situations ranging from parliamentary democracy to tyranny.

3. Therefore truth moves faster than lies, and propaganda becomes flammable.

4. They are not prone to traditional and endemic ideologies: Labourism, Islamism, Fianna Fail Catholicism etc... in fact hermetic ideologies of all forms are rejected.

5. Women very numerous as the backbone of movements. After twenty years of modernised labour markets and higher-education access the "archetypal" protest leader, organizer, facilitator, spokesperson now is an educated young woman.

6. Horizontalism has become endemic because technology makes it easy: it kills vertical hierarchies spontaneously, whereas before – and the quintessential experience of the 20th century – was the killing of dissent within movements, the channeling of movements and their bureaucratisaton.

7. Memes: "A meme acts as a unit for carrying cultural ideas symbols or practices, which can be transmitted from one mind to another through writing, speech, gestures, rituals or other imitable phenomena. Supporters of the concept regard memes as cultural analogues to genes, in that they self-replicate, mutate and respond to selective pressures." (Wikipedia) – so what happens is that ideas arise, are very quickly "market tested" and either take off, bubble under, insinuate themselves or if they are deemed no good they disappear. Ideas self-replicate like genes. Prior to the internet this theory (see Richard Dawkins, 1976) seemed an over-statement but you can now clearly trace the evolution of memes.

8. They all seem to know each other: not only is the network more powerful than the hierarchy – but the ad-hoc network has become easier to form. So if you "follow" somebody from the UCL occupation on Twitter, as I have done, you can easily run into a radical blogger from Egypt, or a lecturer in peaceful resistance in California who mainly does work on Burma so then there are the Burmese tweets to follow. During the early 20th century people would ride hanging on the undersides of train carriages across borders just to make links like these.

9. The specifics of economic failure: the rise of mass access to university-level education is a given. Maybe soon even 50% in higher education will be not enough. In most of the world this is being funded by personal indebtedess – so people are making a rational judgement to go into debt so they will be better paid later. However the prospect of ten years of fiscal retrenchment in some countries means they now know they will be poorer than their parents. And the effect has been like throwing a light switch; the prosperity story is replaced with the doom story, even if for individuals reality will be more complex, and not as bad as they expect.

10. This evaporation of a promise is compounded in the more repressive societies and emerging markets because – even where you get rapid economic growth – it cannot absorb the demographic bulge of young people fast enough to deliver rising living standards for enough of them.

11. To amplify: I can't find the quote but one of the historians of the French Revolution of 1789 wrote that it was *not the product of poor people but of poor lawyers*. You can have political/economic setups that disappoint the poor for generations – but if lawyers, teachers and doctors are sitting in their garrets freezing and starving you get revolution. Now, in their garrets, they have a laptop and broadband connection.

12. The weakness of organised labour means there's a changed relationship between the radicalized middle class, the poor and the organised workforce. The world looks more like 19th century Paris – heavy predomination of the "progressive" intelligentsia, intermixing with the slum-dwellers at numerous social interfaces (cabarets then, raves now); huge social fear of the excluded poor but also many rags to riches stories celebrated in the media (Fifty Cent etc); meanwhile the solidaristic culture and respectability of organized labour is still there but, as in Egypt, they find themselves a "stage army" to be marched on and off the scene of history.

13. This leads to a loss of fear among the young radicals of any movement: they can pick and choose; there is no confrontation they can't retreat from. They can "have a day off" from protesting, occupying: whereas twith he old working-class based movements, their place in the ranks of battle was determined and they couldn't retreat once things started. You couldn't "have a day off" from the miners' strike if you lived in a pit village.

14. In addition to a day off, you can "mix and match": I have met people who do community organizing one day, and the next are on a flotilla to Gaza; then they pop up working for a think tank on sustainable energy; then they're writing a book about something completely different. I was astonished to find people I had interviewed inside the UCL occupation blogging from Tahrir Square this week.

15. People just know more than they used to. Dictatorships rely not just on the suppression of news but on the suppression of narratives and truth.

More or less everything you need to know to make sense of the world is available as freely downloadable content on the internet: and it's not pre-digested for you by your teachers, parents, priests, imams. For example there are huge numbers of facts available to me now about the subjects I studied at university that were not known when I was there in the 1980s. Then whole academic terms would be spent disputing basic facts, or trying to research them. Now that is still true but the plane of reasoning can be more complex because people have an instant reference source for the undisputed premises of arguments. It's as if physics has been replaced by quantum physics, but in every discipline.

16. There is no Cold War, and the War on Terror is not as effective as the Cold War was in solidifying elites against change. Egypt is proving to be a worked example of this: though it is highly likely things will spiral out of control, post Mubarak – as in all the colour revolutons – the dire warnings of the US right that this will lead to Islamism are a "meme" that has not taken off. In fact you could make an interesting study of how the meme starts, blossoms and fades away over the space of 12 days. To be clear: I am not saying they are wrong – only that the fear of an Islamist takeover in Egypt has not been strong enough to swing the US presidency or the media behind Mubarak.

17. It is – with international pressure and some powerful NGOs – possible to bring down a repressive government without having to spend years in the jungle as a guerilla, or years in the urban underground: instead the oppositional youth – both in the west in repressive regimes like Tunisia/ Egypt, and above all in China – live in a virtual undergrowth online and through digital comms networks. The internet is not key here – it is for example the things people swap by text message, the music they swap with each other etc: the hidden meanings in graffiti, street art etc which those in authority fail to spot.

18. People have a better understanding of power. The activists have read their Chomsky and their Hardt-Negri, but the ideas therein have become mimetic: young people believe the issues are no longer class and econom-ics but simply power: they are clever to the point of expertise in knowing how to mess up hierarchies and see the various "revolutions" in their own lives as part of an "exodus" from oppression, not – as previous generations did – as a "diversion into the personal". While Foucault could tell Gilles Deleuze, "We had to wait until the nineteenth century before we began to understand the nature of exploitation, and to this day, we have yet to fully comprehend the nature of power," that's probably changed.

19.   As the algebraic sum of all these factors it feels like the protest "meme" that is sweeping the world – if that premise is indeed true – is profoundly less radical on economics than the one that swept the world in the 1910s and 1920s; they don't seek a total overturn: they seek a moderation of excesses. However on politics the common theme is the dissolution of centralized power and the demand for "autonomy" and personal freedom in addition to formal democracy and an end to corrupt, family based power-elites.

20.   Technology has – in many ways, from the contraceptive pill to the iPod, the blog and the CCTV camera – expanded the space and power of the individual.

SOME COMPLICATIONS...

a)   All of the above are generalisations, and have to be read as such.

b)   Are these methods replicable by their opponents? Clearly up to a point they are. So the assumption in the global progressive movement that their values are aligned with that of the networked world may be wrong. Also we have yet to see what happens to all this social networking if a state ever seriously pulls the plug on the technology: switches the mobile network off, censors the internet, cyber-attacks the protesters.

c)   China is the laboratory here, where the Internet Police are paid to go online and foment pro-government "memes" to counteract the oppositional ones. The Egyptian leftist blogger Arabawy.org says on his website that "in a dictatorship, independent journalism by default becomes a form of activism, and the spread of information is essentially an act of agitation." But independent journalism is suppressed in many parts of the world.

d)   What happens to this new, fluffy global zeitgeist when it runs up against the old-style hierarchical dictatorship in a death match, where the latter has about 300 Abrams tanks? We may be about to find out.

e)   (and this one is troubling for mainstream politics) Are we creating a complete disconnect between the values and language of the state and those of the educated young? Egypt is a classic example – if you hear the NDP officials there is a time-warped aspect to their language compared to that of young doctors and lawyers on the Square. But there are also examples in the UK: much of the political discourse – on both sides of the

House of Commons – is treated by many young people as a barely intelligible "noise" – and this goes wider than just the protesters.

(For example: I'm finding it common among non-politicos these days that whenever you mention the "Big Society" there's a shrug and a suppressed laugh – yet if you move into the warren of thinktanks around Westminster, it's treated deadly seriously. Dissing the Big Society has quickly become a "meme" that crosses political tribal boundaries under the Coalition, yet most professional politicians are deaf to "memes" as the youth are to the contents of Hansard.)

Article originally published at-http://www.bbc.co.uk/blogs/newsnight/paulmason/ 2011/02/twenty_reasons_why_its_kicking.html

Minor Compositions

As well as a multitude to come...